It's Not About the Funeral–
What You Need to Know
Before You Go

Chris R. Bentley

Strategic Book Publishing
New York, New York

Strategic Book Publishing
An imprint of Writers Literary & Publishing Services, Inc.
845 Third Avenue, 6th Floor – 6016
New York, NY 10022
http://www.strategicbookpublishing.com

ISBN: 978-1-60693-660-3, 1-60693-660-3

Printed in the United States of America

Book Design/Layout by: Andrew Herzog

Photo Credits:
Introduction, River View Cemetery, Portland, OR by Author
Chapter I, Irish Wolfhound by Author
Chapter II, La Chacarita Cemetery, Argentina by Author
Chapter III, Sacrificial Bench, Chichen Itza, Mexico by Author
Chapter IV, by permission of Cascade Funeral Directors
Chapter V, Skull sculpture on crematory wall, Chichen Itza, Mexico by Author
Chapter VI, By permission of Cascade Funeral Directors
Chapter VII, La Recoleta Cemetery, Argentina by Author
Chapter VIII, River View Cemetery, Portland, OR by Author
Chapter IX, Isla Mujeras cemetery, Mexico by Author
Chapter X, By permission Cascade Funeral Directors

Dedication

To Connie, the love of my life and soul mate. Her support and encouragement made this a better book.

And to my children, Chris and Jennifer, for filling my days with laughter; my pride knows no boundaries.

Table of Contents

Preface

This book is intended to educate readers about the death care industry. Readers will learn how to arrange for funeral and cemetery services and goods. They will gain not only the knowledge necessary to avoid overspending and emotional stress, but also insights on being a smarter consumer when dealing with an industry about which so little is known. Many death care industry owners and employees are honorable and forthright people. Yet, there are those who are not going to have the consumer's best interests at heart. The consumer of the death care industry services and products sets his own trap. Ignorance of the funeral business allows the industry to knowingly—or sometimes unknowingly—manipulate the consumer.

The author is not a lifelong member of the industry, but a consumer who happened to have worked in the business for over five years. This work is a result of the author's observations and experiences.

"Would you tell me, please, which way I ought to go from here?"

"That depends a good deal on where you want to get to," said the Cat.

"I don't much care where," said Alice.

"Then it doesn't matter which way you go," said the Cat.

—Lewis Carrol, *Alice's Adventures in Wonderland*

Introduction

"What can I know? What should I do? What may I hope for?"
—Immanuel Kant, German philosopher (1724-1804)

Death lies just beyond the horizon for all of us. Death is a tragedy; or at least most deaths are tragic. As sure as the sun will rise, you will die. Maybe it will not happen today or tomorrow, but someday your time will come, and most people are not prepared. I'm not talking spiritually; I'm talking about the nuts and bolts of what the dead and the survivors need. As a former funeral home owner, I relied on that fact.

Dying, funerals, and cemeteries generally are the last things we want to discuss. Our modern culture considers talking about death a taboo. Those who have not benefited from modern electronics, communications, and the ability to prolong life have no such taboos since death is a more common event. However, all of us will need the use of a funeral home. Reality hits when someone in your family dies, the reality that you are not prepared. And when you're not prepared, you make mistakes, mistakes that will cost you money and emotional aggravation.

The funeral industry wants your money. All businesses want your money, but unlike when you buy a car or television set, you won't do your research, and the funeral industry knows this. Most Americans will spend more time agonizing over the placement and cost of a new flat-screen television set than where or how Grandpa is going to be buried. Again, the funeral industry knows that you don't know squat about the funeral industry. You have no idea where to go, what to ask once you're there, and why your seemingly friendly funeral director says what he says. But the funeral director, sometimes known as a funeral service provider, knows what to say and, if he's good, how to manipulate a family in order to bring the big bucks home. You will have no idea what has happened to you. You may even think that you were fairly treated and that your funeral director, or pre-need salesperson, was kind and sympathetic.

Most funeral homes are privately held; however, one person or a group of owners may hold one to twenty or so homes. These are the independent funeral homes. On the other hand, large corporations own many funeral homes and cemeteries. The "big boys" are Service Corp. International (SCI), Alderwood Group (which at the time of this writing had recently been bought out by SCI), and Stewart Enterprises. Most of the large corporations in the funeral business also owe large, sometimes unimaginable, sums of money to their bankers. The big three corporations, and some of the smaller ones, went on a buying spree in the eighties and nineties. They bought funeral homes and cemeteries, and borrowed millions upon millions to make those purchases. However, they made some very big mistakes. First, the big companies paid way too much for these properties. Second, the death rate didn't climb as they predicted. Now, the larger funeral corporations owe their bankers billions. It's so bad that, in some cases, they have sold some of the properties back to the original owners. They're in trouble, but you won't know it from the outside looking in. Many of their sales and marketing tactics are motivated by their financial problems.

SCI is the biggest funeral home and cemetery owner in the world. According to their 2007 annual report, SCI's total assets amounted to over $8 billion, of which almost $2 billion of that was "goodwill," whatever that means. However, SCI's total liabilities were over $2 billion. Guess who's going to pay those liabilities? Not the good fairy, but you, should you ever decide to use a SCI facility. How will you know if you are dealing with a large corporation as opposed to an independently owned funeral home? You won't—because you won't ask. Sure, there is a small sign at the door informing you of the true owner. But when you walk into Joe Smith's Funeral home at the time of a death, you think that Joe Smith is running the place, and this is probably not true. Furthermore, corporate-held funeral homes tend to be more expensive than independently held homes.

Should you go to a funeral home owned by, say SCI, and ask who owns the funeral home, they will tell you SCI. But they will also say that they are independently run. What that means is that the managers of such homes have some latitude when it comes to pricing and practices. But, when they start to negotiate pricing, the corporation that owns the home will fix a floor price that the management cannot go below. Independent funeral homes have much more latitude; therefore, you have much more negotiating power. It is a rare thing to find a privately held, single funeral home these days. However, many funeral home owners and funeral directors will not rip you off in your time of need. They will sell to you what you want and what is needed by law, not what you don't want or don't need. Unfortunately, it's up to you, the consumer, to find someone you are comfortable with and trust.

When we walk into a funeral home or go to a cemetery to make arrangements for ourselves or for a loved one, we are naïve. We ask ourselves what do we know and what should we do? Our confusion is not generated by a lack of intelligence, but by a lack of education. We don't know because we don't want to know. We don't know what to do because for most of our lives we had no need to deal with a funeral home or cemetery. We don't know what to hope for because we have no aspirations.

How do I know all of the things that go on in the funeral business? Well, I worked for a funeral home combined with a cemetery (known as a combo unit) for two-and-a-half years. Then I resigned, started my own funeral home, and ran it for over three years. During this period, I made it my business to study the funeral industry. This journey began because of personal experiences. Like most of you, I had no idea what the death care industry was about, much less how it ran. Like most people, I started as an observer, attending other family's funeral services.

Then I became a consumer, arranging the service and burial of a loved one. Finally, I became a participant in the industry.

Not surprisingly, I found that being ripped off, disappointed, and unsatisfied by the funeral home or cemetery you choose is less likely if you educate yourself and shop around. Pick the funeral home/cemetery you feel most comfortable with and know what's behind the talk.

Chapter I

To End You Must Begin

Most people have a certain fascination with death and the process of death. We all want to look at the picture of the dead person lying in the street after an auto accident. We slow our cars down and rubberneck hoping to see the damage and blood. At Aunt Gertrude's funeral, we will look in the casket and perhaps touch her just to see what death feels like. But we just want a slight brush of death; we don't want to know everything because death scares the daylights out of almost all of us. And we certainly don't want to know the details about how Aunt Gertrude made it from the nursing home to that casket.

My first experience with death was during the 1960s when a friend's mother died of a massive stroke, and I went to the funeral. It was a nice chapel service, but there was no casket. She had been cremated, and her urn was placed on a pedestal next to the podium. I was very disappointed because I was hoping to view the body. I was bored; no body, no fun. The next service I attended was a memorial service. Again, no body. But this service was for a high school friend of mine who spent four years on the cross-country and track team. He was lost at sea—literally—during my first year in college. After graduating from high school, he worked on a commercial fishing boat in the Pacific Northwest, and died. It was reported that one minute he was on deck; the next, he was gone. The family paid a funeral home to run the service. Then, during the first couple of years in college, I became an ambulance attendant and driver. This was before paramedics were around who were able to communicate with local emergency rooms, use defibrillators, and start IVs. We just tried to stop the bleeding, performed CPR, strapped the injured in, and transported the patient. Yet even in this capacity, death was rare. And if death occurred, the pronouncement was made after we had delivered to the emergency room, so my exposure was minimal.

Then I got a real taste of death. During my last year of college, I took a job as a pathology technician. My main duty was to assist in autopsy, and I loved the job. I was finishing my degree in Clinical Sciences, and my desire at the time was to become a physician. I'm glad that I never made it to medical school, and I think that most of my potential patients are glad I didn't make it also. But at the time, it fit my goals and I learned a lot. I learned anatomy; I learned that dead people don't care about anything; I learned that some had had a hard life and that some had suffered severe pain until the end. However, the biggest lesson I learned was that dead people smelled, especially on the inside. When we did a post-mortem, I always hoped the body had been in the cooler for a couple of hours before the procedure. I almost lost my cookies on my first postmortem. The guy had an obstructed bowel and when we opened him up, his intestines sprung forth like a bunch of long balloons let loose from a container. After that experience, nothing bothered me.

Upon graduation from college, I had little connection with death except during my stint as a dialysis technician, and there, death was a very rare thing. During my time as a dialysis tech, I found that making money was more important than trying to go to med school. Besides, I reasoned, I would probably flunk out or end up killing people. So for the next twenty-five years or so, I was out of medicine and away from death. That is, until my father died.

When my father died, it was the first time I, as a survivor and an emotional, at-need customer, had to deal with a funeral director. My father's death was sudden, but I knew he was going to die since he had looked like death the last time I saw him. His death cut me to the core. And because we as a family were unprepared, we paid for our naïveté.

It was a simple service—immediate family and two others attended, nine people in all. We paid for two grave spaces, one for him and one for my mother because, as we were told by the cemetery sales guy, that space next to my father may not be available when it was mother's time, and this was true. The funeral director sold us a bronze casket because of my father's "position in the community" and because "he would like it." *Like it? He was dead!* We also purchased a Monticello burial vault which we didn't need, but the cemetery sales guy told us that we needed to protect that very nice casket. *From what?* He tried to sell us a bronze burial vault to match the bronze casket, which cost five times the Monticello, but we didn't bite. What fries me to this day is that I, as a layperson, had to arrange for the military honor guard, something that was very difficult. That arrangement was actually the funeral director's job, but he was too lazy to do it and told me that if I wanted one, I would have to arrange for it myself.

We got hammered because we didn't know, we didn't shop around, and we didn't do our homework. We were in shock, and the salespeople knew it and took advantage of the situation. Since my father's death, I have dealt three separate times with that funeral home and cemetery combo unit, but in those subsequent times, I have been prepared, and it has made all the difference.

I entered the funeral business upon the impending death of my dog. Our Irish wolfhound, the best damn dog you can have, was suffering from a sarcoma of his left front leg. He weighed two hundred pounds.

Now, all but two of our pets who have passed away reside in our backyard. But the thought of digging a hole big enough for a two-hundred pound dog was daunting, so we decided we would cremate the dog after we put him down. Our twenty-year-old cockatiel is being stuffed as I write this, and I am aggrieved by the cost. But that's a different story.

So, my wife bought a Celtic-looking jar from Pier One Imports to contain the remains of our good and loyal dog when the time came. But she's a shopper, and wanted to see a more formal urn from a funeral home. After all, the dog was bigger than many humans, and, therefore, a real urn seemed like it might be more suitable.

Down we went to the local funeral home/cemetery combo unit on a Sunday to look at urns. There, we met a nice lady who was delighted to show (and sell) us an urn for our dog. I was shocked by the prices. Their urns where priced from a sixty dollar piece of junk I wouldn't use for anyone's dog's remains to a three thousand dollar acrylic monstrosity. We said no to all. The dog now resides in the Pier One Imports Celtic jar.

As my wife was looking over their display, however, I began to chat with the salesperson about her job. She told me it was a great job because you got to set your own hours more or less and the pay was great and the funeral home was always looking for good "pre-need" salespeople. Having been out of work for about a year by choice, I was intrigued. My wife wanted me out of the house, and I didn't mind the thought of making a little extra money. The salesperson set an appointment with her sales manager for the following week. I went and started a real education.

My "interview" with the sales manager was the twilight zone of interviews. Now, I have been interviewed before, and I have interviewed others; but I have never ended up having the job literally pushed on me. The sales manager just glanced at my résumé, and the only thing that interested him was the fact that I was college educated. When I've been interviewed, or I have interviewed someone, it's been about qualifications, education level, personality, and what assets the person is going to bring to the table. In the interview at the funeral home, it was about how much money could be made, and how easy it would be to bring big checks home. I could work when I wanted. He didn't care that I had never held a sales job; he just wanted a warm body to sell cemetery services and funerals. Of course, I was hired.

What did I know about the death care industry? As a new pre-need salesman, I needed to understand "at-need," "pre-need," and my role in the operation. Here are some definitions and examples of what I as a salesman needed to know.

A client who calls or walks into a funeral home or mortuary seeking information or arrangements for the care of a deceased person is an at-need client. Because of a death, this client needs services immediately. Someone who inquires about services for himself or for anyone else who is still alive is considered a pre-need client. I had people come to me saying that their mother was hours away from the grim reaper. But the grim reaper is sometimes late and does not show up until months later. A pre-need client turns to an at-need client the moment a person dies. And there is a big difference on how the funeral home will handle pre-need and at-need clients.

In the mortuary, funeral, and cemetery sales business, there are two actors. First is the funeral director or the "funeral services practitioner," who deals with those families arranging the final disposition of a decedent. A funeral director is responsible for handling and deposing the dead. You may deal with a director, assistant director or an intern director in training, but a licensed funeral director is the responsible person when caring for the dead. The second is the family services counselor or pre-need salesperson. Combo units that have a cemetery and attached funeral home will divide sales in two parts: (a) funeral services and merchandise sales and (b) cemetery and merchandise sales. In an at-need situation, the funeral director and the family services counselor will divide the sale of the funeral and cemetery, forming a "tag team." This allows the funeral director to concentrate on the funeral and the family services counselor to devote his or her time to arranging the actual burial. In reality, this arrangement just adds to the confusion of the customer. The client is now not dealing with one "expert" but two, and how can you argue with two experts? The tag team is also designed to wear you down by extending the arrangement. Some places don't use this tag team, such as stand-alone funeral homes, but most combo units do. Let's go into the character and duties of the salesperson first.

The salesperson or the family services counselor is also sometimes called a "cemeterian." Doesn't that sound like a well-trained, certified, helpful professional? Well, for the most part, that is not the case. Sure this person is licensed by most states, but licensure is just a cursory background check and the payment of fees. Most of the "family services counselors" that I've met are poorly educated, nonprofessional, ill trained, and slovenly. These people just happen to qualify for the job because they can breathe. They can't find other jobs and are not educated for the most part; therefore, the company does not want to spend the time or money to train them properly. Many of these people haven't an ethical bone in their bodies, but they're desperate; and desperate people are dangerous to your wallet.

The major obstacles a pre-need salesperson faces is that most people under the age of sixty-five will not prearrange for their final disposition, it's just a subject people don't want to think or talk about. However, as age creeps up on us, there are a few who will plan their final arrangements in order to get what they want, take the burden off their children, or just because they are planners. The only duty of a mortuary/funeral home/cemetery salesperson is to sell—not what you want or need, but as much as you're willing to buy. And that salesperson won't give a rat's rear end about your desires or the effect it will have on your pocketbook. Why? Because in all likelihood, the salesperson is on a commission-only basis, which leads to a conflict of interest. The salesperson is not interested in your needs, but only in his needs. You don't buy; he doesn't eat. The more you buy, the fatter his wallet.

On the other hand, there are some ethical, thoughtful, educated, and professional salespeople within the industry who really enjoy the work. I know I did. These people will try to do the right thing by you. But they can be hard to find, especially in the corporate-held funeral homes. You'll likely come across a more honest salesperson in a privately held, small funeral home.

That's why corporate-owned funeral homes and cemeteries don't care who they hire. They figure if they have enough bodies making one hundred phone calls a day, then someone's going to buy something. The corporations don't care that since they have hired so many commission salespeople there aren't enough sales to go around. The sales department within a funeral home fosters an atmosphere of nonprofessional attitudes, deceit, lies, hate, secrecy, and disharmony among the sales force. An unprofessional attitude that generates theft by deception means the customer is the victim. This happens not because corporations owning these funeral homes want such an atmosphere, but because that's the way the sales system is. It can happen in the smaller funeral homes too; but the staffs aren't as big, and the problems are more contained.

Think about it. You're a salesperson on a payment of one hundred percent commissions; you need to make sales to keep hearth and home and job. In the sales office there is a tote board tracking every sale you've made, and there is a set goal. And God help you if you miss your goal three times in a row, or fewer times in other places. The sales manager can replace you in a day with some other schmuck off the street, and the company's cost is minimal. Not all funeral homes, also known as mortuaries, are run as stated above; but some are. It's up to you, the consumer, to either avoid such places or at least know what's going on before you fork over your hard-earned cash.

I joined a sales staff of just four other people: two women, one man, and the sales manager. I was handed a large stack of cards with the names, addresses, and phone numbers of people who desired either cremation or burial. You know this gimmick. Fill out the survey and qualify to win a Caribbean cruise! The company doesn't actually care about the survey. When you fill out one of these cards, you've just provided the company with a sales lead. My task for the day was to call one hundred of these people and see if I could get them in to buy cemetery property. The survey cards give the salesperson a reason to call. I was given a script that was designed as a sales tool to lead the prospect toward the "right" decision. The script was so bad it seemed as if an eighth grader with English as a second language had written it. Reading the script was my "training."

Officially, I had a three month probation/training period. I would receive a small stipend that would increase every two weeks. Should I sell anything, my commission would go not to me, but into my commission reserve (topping out at two thousand dollars) in case I had any cancellations. This was a nice way to pay me very little while making money on my commission reserve until the day I died, quit, or was fired. In order to fill my commission reserve, I needed a minimum of twenty thousand dollars in sales. It's not the same everywhere. Some places, the commission starts low; and as you gain sales over a period of time, your commission increases. This is a big incentive to do well in the job, a big incentive to commit fraud.

I made those one hundred phone calls on my first day. The responses I heard ranged from, "No thank you, I'm not interested" to "You want to sell what? Don't call this number again or I'll tear your head off!" Needless to say, I didn't make any sales that day. I remember one call in particular where it turned out that the person filling out the information on our little cards for the cruise was only sixteen. When I called, I had reached the mother who wanted to know why I was calling and couldn't understand why I was trying to sell her daughter a cremation niche in our cemetery. The girl's mother went nuts.

Thousands of those cards had been filled out. However, these people didn't want to talk about their impending death. They wanted a chance at a Caribbean cruise. Still, our company got thousands of phone numbers and almost every one of those numbers was called—again and again and again until the person who made the mistake of giving his or her number either gave in and finally bought something or threatened some action to make us stop calling. Remember, once you give someone in the funeral industry your phone number, you have a buddy for life until you either threaten him/her or buy. If you do buy, once he/she has milked you for all he/she can get, you will never hear from him/her unless that salesperson can figure out another way to drag more money from you. By the way, that Caribbean cruise was indeed given away, but those cards were distributed nationally by the corporate headquarters, so your chance of winning was about one in a million.

After a couple of days of this, I started to separate those cards into call, don't call. A few of the cards actually had, "I need to think about this," or "Please call." It got so that I would look at the handwriting to decipher whether or not to call a certain card's phone number! It was like trying to decipher the intentions of a voter when looking at a hanging chad on a voting ballot. I actually got some sales off of those cards. But those sales took months to close because picking out your funeral arrangements and where you're going to be buried is not a high priority for most people.

Of course, there are only so many Caribbean cruise cards to go through, and I threw about three-fourths of them away. "Next up," my sales manager said, "open the phone book and start calling." My reaction? No way! I was not about to pester people out of the blue for something they didn't want, just as I don't want to be pestered out of the blue from someone selling me something I don't want.

Let's go into what a salesperson at a combo unit does to earn his or her keep. The salesperson's main function is to sell. However, most salespeople will deny that they sell and instead claim to be just presenting "informed choices" to each customer. In other words, beat the customer over the head with the "memorializing and honoring" velvet hammer.

Most combo units will have a pre-need salesperson and an at-need salesperson on duty. All inquiries for services and merchandise for people who haven't died go to the pre-need salesperson. That person's job is to answer phone inquiries, get appointments from those inquiries, and deal with walk-in customers.

The pre-need salesperson on duty dreams of your phone inquiry and salivates over your unexpected appearance at the facility because he knows that he has a hot prospect. A voluntary phone call or walk-in is a more easily acquired lead than cold calling or door knocking. He will tell you how wise you are to prearrange because you're locking in the cost and saving your children from unnecessary decision-making and financial costs. He will be soft spoken and understanding of your needs and desires; he will note what kind of car you drive. He will agree with you that you don't want any unnecessary expenses, all the while nudging you toward more expensive merchandise and services. Should you call for an appointment, he will be available at any time, any day, at your home or the establishment's facility. He will even pick you up in his car just to make it easier for you.

He'll try to get you to come to him since it's easier to sell you more in the facility where he works, but he'll come to your home if necessary and will bring nice pictures of merchandise. He really wants you in the facility, however, because if you actually see the product and can touch the merchandise, you're more likely to buy. He knows you're nibbling at the bait; he wants a chance to set the hook. Lastly, he has your name and number, and you will be hearing from him until you either relent and buy or tell him to get lost.

He wants and needs to know whether you desire burial or cremation. This is important to both the salesperson and you. A burial will cost more, and cremation considerably less. If you choose cremation, he will ask why and attempt to steer you towards burial. He will play on your guilt, emotions, and ignorance to get you to bury instead of cremate. He will use the honoring and memorializing playbook to get you to buy more and do more. Why? The more goods and services he sells to you, the bigger a commission he gets. But if you choose cremation, he will still be your "understanding friend" and will make money. Your salesperson is a tour guide "informing" you of the choices of products and services you can buy whether you choose cremation or burial.

Sales leads are treated like gold and are closely guarded by the individual salesperson who developed the lead. Why? Sales leads are stolen by other salespeople all the time. If a salesperson drops the ball on a potential client, that lead may be fair game. Remember, the salesperson has to make monthly sales goals and has to feed a family. He or she will do anything to get a good lead, including cheating or stealing. Going through another salesperson's desk and files is a common practice. The company culture is tense and deceptive, and you should be aware and wary. There are never enough sales to justify the number of sales staff. These people are desperate.

Almost all the costs of merchandise and services you arrange for in a pre-need situation become fixed from the time you sign the sales contract. There are a few exceptions. Say you want to put money aside for flowers, an organist, or death certificates. The cost of these items may, over time, increase, and your family will have to pay the difference since the funeral home can't control these costs by adjusting their printed price lists. Again, these are items such as death certificates, flowers, permits, etc., charged to the funeral home by other vendors or a government agency. Therefore, if you prearranged and included two death certificates at fifteen dollars apiece, but you didn't use that service for twenty years, those death certificates may now cost twenty dollars apiece, and your family will have to cough up the difference. These items are what are known in the industry and listed on the Statement of Goods and Services as "cash advanced items."

Additionally, there are still some mortuaries and cemeteries that don't have "guaranteed sales" prearrangement contracts. I would not sign and pay for any prearrangements without a "guaranteed sales" contract. Fixing the price of services and merchandise is a major reason for prearrangement. For example, a gentleman whose wife passed away twenty years ago bought and paid for both her funeral and burial and his. But his prearrangement did not guarantee the price. Therefore, when he died, relatives had to come up with the difference between the price twenty years ago and today.

The pre-need salesperson doesn't care if you put money down on cash advanced items. He won't get any commission from such goods because the funeral home doesn't control those items. He wants to sell you the "goods," the hard stuff, which is where the real money is. We'll go over "cash advanced items" later.

But back to the beginning. When I started working for a large funeral corporation, my boss gave me a good sales lead. A husband and wife wanted to bury at our combo unit since they had received in the mail a twenty percent discount coupon that they could use against cemetery property if they acted soon. The trouble was, they could not speak English, and I couldn't speak their language. Plus, they were dirt poor. I had to go to their home since they had no transportation, and they did not want me to take them to the funeral home because it scared them silly. But they were getting on in years, and the husband had some serious health problems, so they insisted that their arrangements be done. And they wanted it all. This kind of lead is a salesperson's dream: two cemetery packages and two full funeral services all tied up in a bow with large commissions to drool over.

I didn't want to do this. Besides the language problem, which made it very hard to communicate, this couple just plain could not afford two funeral services and two gravesites. Since they were insistent, I tried to steer them toward simple direct cremations, which to them was out of the question. I then tried to persuade them to purchase part of the package, say for instance just the gravesites. No, they wanted everything arranged, right down to the final inscription on their marker.

All funeral homes and cemeteries will finance without credit check on any purchase; and the down payment is up to the customer, which makes the purchase less painful—initially. However, the interest for the most part is twelve percent, and in most cases you have sixty months to pay off the financing. Some places will refund the interest if you pay off the contract within twelve months, but most people can't afford to pay the contract so quickly. Also, if you don't pay your monthly bill on time, there are penalty charges. Should you cease payment altogether, you lose all the money and items that you have paid to the funeral home or cemetery.

Because of the ability for customers to easily finance cemetery and funeral arrangements, the above family was able to make their final arrangements. I was not happy to be a party to this sale. However, since I worked for a large corporation, I was able to make their funeral arrangements and all their cemetery merchandise through another funeral home that the corporation owned which had lower prices than the facility were I worked. The couple would be buried at the combo facility where I worked, but that facility would only receive payment for graves and the opening and closing of those graves when the time came. The other funeral home would receive all the monies for the funeral services, grave liner, marker and caskets—all at a significantly reduced price to my customers who, unfortunately, still really could not afford what they wanted.

So, the down payment was made, and the contracts signed. I made sure that the couple's children were present since they spoke better English than their parents. It was important to me they all understood what they were getting into. Most pre-need salespeople would have cared less whether or not their potential clients could afford the products and merchandise in question. For such salespeople, the motivation is only quotas and commissions. They would have walked into this couple's home, sold them funeral packages and cemetery property, had them sign the contracts, and then taken their money without so much as letting the door hit them in the fanny on their way out.

"But," you might say, "you're a hypocrite. You know there are other funeral homes that are even cheaper than the one you used for this poor family. Why didn't you send them to one of your competitors, maybe to an independent funeral home?" And yes, I could have done so, but this family insisted on using their coupon, by God, and use it they did. They, like most customers, did not shop around. There was no research. They had no idea what it was going to cost and what they had to buy in order to receive the services they wanted. It took me two weeks to get the corporate types to allow me to use the coupon at the other funeral home. In addition, I had to twist the arm of the manager at the other funeral home to accept the coupon, which in turn lowered his prices. I was not going to shop around for this family. That was their responsibility. Plus, I had a responsibility to my employer. Even though I hoped and urged this family to be wise enough not to prearrange, they were insistent. At that point, it was my duty to sell my employer's products and services not those of our competitors. The company I worked for was, in fact, overpriced. This family should have realized what they could afford was a simple direct cremation from someone else; and if their religion or beliefs prevented cremation, they should have shopped around and arranged—but not paid for—what they wanted. Then later a collection could have been taken up within their family or church.

The whole point of the story is to shop, compare, and learn. Don't buy what you can't afford. A good option for those who have little money but are thinking about prearrangement is to buy pieces of the services and merchandise. In other words, buy a gravesite, and after paying the gravesite off, buy the funeral. Then proceed to the merchandise. The above family was lucky I handled them because my coworkers would have done nothing to lower the price. If a pre-need salesperson gets any cash— and I've seen one hundred dollar down payments on services amounting to over eight thousand dollars—he or she will take the money without any thought as to how you're going to pay off the rest of the contract. Anyone who can only put down such a small amount on such a large service probably won't be able to pay it off and will lose their money. Should a customer stop or fail to make payments on his or her contract, the company's corporate home office will notify the salesperson that the commission is in jeopardy. The salesperson will in turn call the customer and warn of the dire consequences should the customer fail to make a payment or seek to cancel the contract.

So what do pre-need salespeople actually sell? Everything they can. If they are working at a funeral home without an attached cemetery, they can prearrange and sell all funeral services, cemetery, and merchandise items except the gravesite and the opening and closing of the grave itself. If they work at a combo unit, as I did, they will sell funeral services, cemetery, merchandise, plus the dirt that comes with it. Prearranged sales are broken into two major categories. The first is cemetery interment sites and merchandise. The second is funeral services and merchandise.

All funeral homes and cemeteries are required to give you price lists as soon as you state your interest in either funeral services or cemetery gravesites. Once a funeral service is mentioned, a general price list must be handed over to the customer before any price is quoted. This is a Federal Trade Commission (FTC) rule, and a violation of the rule is costly to the salesperson and the company for which he or she works. The rule does not apply to phone contact for obvious reasons.

Chapter II

Pre-Need Cemetery Sales

An Exercise in Hammering the Customer

There are many forms of permanent internment within a cemetery; from full body ground burial to commingling of cremated remains in a hidden common columbarium. In order to understand all the choices presented to the pre-need customer, dividing this chapter into sections seems appropriate.

The Cemetery

The word *cemetery* is derived from the Greek word meaning *sleeping place*. Very appropriate. A cemetery is a place where bodies and cremated remains are interred. The advent of graveyards came into being in Europe around the seventh century. Locations of graveyards were consecrated grounds of a church. With the increased population and death rates due to infectious diseases during the industrial revolution, graveyards were discontinued, sometimes outlawed; and cemeteries sprung up outside city limits. One of the earliest landscaped cemeteries is the Père Lachaise in Paris, France. These changes took burial from church control to state control. Such changes also allowed for the rise of private, for-profit cemeteries.

Your elderly Aunt Mildred has asked you to look into arrangements for her at your local funeral home/cemetery combined unit, because, after all, she has realized that she won't live forever. When you go to your favorite cemetery or memorial park to inquire into a burial, mausoleum or urn space, you need to realize you're not actually buying that physical property. You are, however, buying the right to inter the remains of any person you allow to be interred within that space. Burial spaces come in many forms, from a full-body burial in the ground to the placement of cremated remains into a columbarium. The options concerning interment within any space you choose are varied. But you can bury anyone you wish in the space you bought as long as you have the right to bury that person and as long as that person is dead.

Should you opt for full ground burial, you need a gravesite. In cemeteries, the cost of a gravesite will vary depending on the location of your plot. Cemeteries are divided into sections or gardens. These sections are often named something like the "Garden of the Good Shepherd," "Garden of Hope," "Eagles," and so on. Usually, the higher up the hill or the better the view, the more expensive the gravesite will be. When choosing a gravesite, no matter how nice the view, when Aunt Mildred dies, she won't see the view. But you may want to consider your family. Some families visit the graves of their loved ones often. Over time, however, visits by families will be less frequent and over the generations, nonexistent.

A single gravesite for an adult will measure three feet by seven feet by four to six feet deep. That's it, nothing special, but the grave is surveyed down to the inch because there is no space between gravesites. The cemetery wants to fit as many gravesites onto its property as possible. The main cost of a cemetery is not the property but the cost of the survey for each plot. The cemetery has large lot maps, sometimes called garden maps, where each gravesite is marked and numbered. Don't bother calling a cemetery and asking for a price list. Ask for a price range because there can be so many different prices within the cemetery that all you would get is about thirty pages of prices that you can't decipher. The cemetery knows this, and it's a way to get you to come to them in order to understand what the prices mean and have a look around.

Your salesperson will take you out to the cemetery where you will be treated to a "drive around." This is where he or she will give you a tour of the cemetery by car. First she will drive by the medium-priced gravesites, next the least desirable locations, then the most expensive locations, and last, the medium-priced locations. This is a little sales trick. First you will drive through a portion of the cemetery that will be what you more or less expected. Then you will see a "garden" which will be low priced because it has some undesirable element to it—bad view, poor drainage, very steep hillside—something that will tend to make you think that this is not what you want. Next you will go to the high roller portion of the cemetery where the views are wonderful. That's why they want more for those sites. But you are thinking, "My God, that's a lot of money for a six-by-seven piece of ground!" Last, you will tour the medium-priced sites again. Not quite the views way up the hill, but nice and less expensive and less painful. Most people will buy in the medium-priced gardens. You can have your salesperson stop the car anywhere in the cemetery and wander to your heart's content, but you're more than likely going to choose the medium-priced gravesite.

I know this trick works because I've done it. When a customer comes in and says, "I want to buy cemetery space, but I don't want to spend very much; show me the cheapest you have," no salesperson will just take the customer to the low priced gardens of the cemetery. The customer is going to get the full tour. In my experience, over fifty percent of the time those people who wanted cheap will buy in the medium price portion of the cemetery. Another little trick is the "favorite garden" trick. The salesperson will say which garden is his favorite. He or she will offer this little tidbit in order to get you thinking, "Well, if that's his favorite garden, there must be a reason." The salesperson might not use this ruse until you've decided on a garden plot. Then she might tell you that you've chosen a site in her favorite garden, just to make you feel warm and cozy with your decision. The idea is that it will make you feel comfortable and more willing to listen to her suggestions on other items.

So, you'll wander around a garden that you think is nice and appropriate and then stand on the spot you want. While you are doing this, you will probably try to avoid stepping on the markers in the grass out of respect. There is no need for this. If you avoid stepping on the markers, you're instead stepping on the deceased bodies. They're dead, though, and don't mind at all. Anyway, you'll stand on a spot you like and the salesperson will check the garden map he's carrying to see if the spot is already taken. If it is, you get to seek out another spot. If it isn't, you get to pay. By the way, the salesperson will always say that you have made an excellent choice.

The salesperson will want to get you back into the office and write up a contract for the gravesite. But maybe you're hesitant and want to think about this; or perhaps you did this without your spouse, and you want him or her to look at the space before you buy. The salesperson will be disappointed but will not show it. He will tell you that perhaps you're right in discussing this with your spouse. He will also tell you that the price is going up soon; the spaces where you want to be buried are going very fast, there is another customer interested in the same space you chose, or something of that nature to scare and motivate you to buy that space as soon as possible. If you don't buy right away, he will reserve the space for a period of time (usually two weeks), so you can think about it and discuss it with your loved ones.

A reserved space is just that. The space you picked out is reserved for you for a designated period of time, and will not be sold to any other party until the reservation time has run out. It also hooks you in as a particular salesperson's lead that no one else can touch. Your salesperson will call you about every two to three days to remind you that time is running out and that "there are others who want that very spot." However, on rare occasions another salesperson might accidentally sell that space to another party because he or she failed to check the reserved spaces postings in the sales office. Every once in a while, a mistake like this will happen because a salesperson simply doesn't care. He has a customer who really wants that space and is willing to put money down as soon as the papers can be drawn up. There are no ethics between commissioned salespeople, and a hard sale is a hard sale.

Should your reserved spot be sold out from under you during the reservation period, you're in luck, because then you can wring concessions from the salesperson you're dealing with by complaining and moaning. The salesperson will be so desperate to get your business that he will voluntarily knock the price down on a space near your reserved spot or throw in some other needed merchandise. That's right, I said *needed* merchandise.

You are not done just because you have bought a gravesite. There is much more to do and purchase. Okay, you're sitting down with your friendly cemetery salesperson, and he has written the contract for sale to you for that space. He will not total the purchase because he's going to sell you more. And you'll eventually need it. Remember, you're in a pre-need sales situation, and your salesperson wants to sell all that you want and all that you will need right there and then. The salesperson doesn't care if you live for two months or fifty years more. He wants all the sales associated with the gravesite you have settled on. If you don't buy the extras now or your family has to buy them later, that salesperson might not be there to get the sale.

Since you've decided on ground burial for Aunt Mildred, you're going to need an outer burial container. This container is designed to do two things: (1) keep the dirt placed above your earthly remains from sinking into the gravesite, and (2) protect the casket that's placed within the container. There is no law that I know of that requires you to have an outer burial container. However, very few cemeteries will allow you to bury without the use of an outer burial container. I personally don't know of any cemetery that will bury just a casket without an outer container, unless the cemetery allows for green burials. I'll get into green burials later.

Outer burial containers come in many styles, and your salesperson is going to sell you the most expensive one you can tolerate. The cheapest is what is called in the trade—you guessed it—an outer burial container, a liner, or grave liner. This container is made out of concrete and is just a flat-lidded box into which the casket is lowered at the time of burial. I highly recommend this container. Yes, it will not hold out water or dirt, but it serves the purpose; and once Aunt Mildred is buried, it doesn't matter to her—she's dead. This is the outer container the salesperson will not show you or have a picture of or sell to you, but it's on the price list.

However, water and dirt on your Aunt Mildred's casket might matter a great deal to you; hence, the burial vault is just the ticket. These outer burial containers come in several styles. They weigh a ton. The lid itself weighs eight hundred pounds and is indeed durable. After the casket is lowered into the vault, which is hanging over the gravesite but not completely lowered, the lid is placed on the vault. The lid has a sticky rubber-like sealing compound, which along with all that weight does a good job of sealing the vault. The basic vault (your choice of color) is painted concrete with a vinyl liner on the inside to make the vault more water-resistant. On all vaults, you get your name, birth and death years, and an emblem such as a rose, cross, wreath, or the like. The vault companies warrant their vaults against breakage or leaks for a number of years. The more expensive the vault, the longer the warranty against damage to the vault under normal usage. It's a safe warranty since I don't know of anyone who has dug up their Aunt Mildred just to check on the condition of the burial vault bought five years ago.

As you go up in price, the vaults become a little heavier and the outsides a little fancier. The big difference is the interior. A notch above the basic burial vaults, there are vaults lined in a hard plastic-like material. Again, this is to resist water intrusion. There are also stainless steel interiors that both resist water and do not corrode. There are copper interiors, too, although I have no idea what advantage copper has over stainless steel except for looks. And finally, the granddaddy of them all, the bronze-lined interior. Very nice, very expensive.

Remember the "drive around" you got when picking your gravesite? Well, the same thing will happen to you when you pick out merchandise. First you're shown an example of a medium- priced vault, then a high-priced one, then the basic one, and then back again to the medium. The salesperson will tell you the advantages of each, but he will not show you a picture of a simple grave liner. Salespeople don't want to sell you a grave liner; they want to sell you a vault, but, remember, that grave liner will be on a price list unless you are in an all vault cemetery, which is a cemetery that will only allow burial vaults. I wouldn't use such a cemetery because if they restrict the use of grave liners, what else will they require of you that may not be necessary? You want to have freedom of choice and not to be hammered with high-priced merchandise. Get the grave liner.

I sold one bronze-lined burial vault. I tried to dissuade the customer from this choice; but his mother had died, and he wanted the same ceremony and merchandise as the funeral home sold to his mother at the time of his father's death. I showed him our cheapest vault and explained in words of one syllable that the less expensive vault would look almost as nice as the bronze vault and would perform just as well. In addition, he and those coming to the graveside service would only see the vault for approximately half an hour, and most wouldn't even notice the vault. But his father had a bronze vault and his mother was going to get a bronze vault in spite of the fact that the bronze vault cost him over four thousand dollars more than the vault I tried to sell to him.

A few cemeteries allow very inexpensive vaults made of plastic. I know they are cheap, and I have heard that they easily crack. They are not very popular to my knowledge, but you might look into using one of those types of vaults if the cemetery allows it. After all, if it breaks after the service when the dead person is buried would you know or care?

So, you think you're done with this nice gravesite and burial vault you just bought? Think again. Next you need a marker or headstone. Remember, in memorial parks they generally allow only flat markers. In cemeteries you can opt for a flat marker or an upright headstone (tombstone). Some places will have separate sections for both and will call themselves or should call themselves, memorial park and cemetery.

Now things start to get messy. Markers and headstones are personalized merchandise, a way of leaving your mark on the world. The cemetery or memorial park will have its own rules and regulations. These rules and regulations are of each cemetery or memorial park's choosing, and vary from place to place. Flat grass markers can come in either bronze or granite. Marble is not sold as in the past because marble is relatively soft and will wear rapidly. Bronze markers are generally more expensive and take longer to deliver. Some places have restricted gardens within the cemetery that allow only bronze markers whereas the rest of the cemetery may be mixed.

With granite flat grass markers, your choices will have to do with size (it matters), color, and the cemetery's regulations. Your pre-need salesperson will want to sell the largest, most colorful marker available. He or she will have samples of markers and each stone type and color on display. Sizes are restricted by the individual cemetery, so there are minimum and maximum sizes. Overall, you can get a marker ranging from twelve by twenty-four inches to a full ledger that covers the entire gravesite. Some cemeteries require a concrete border that may or may not be included in the price. If your Aunt Mildred is married and has chosen two spaces side by side, you will at least consider a double marker that covers the top of both spaces. This is usually more economical than buying two separate stones. The stone's color will have a huge bearing on the price. True, some colors are less common, and a granite quarry will charge more, but the up-charge is ridiculous. The most costly part of a stone is the polishing, and all stones are polished no matter what color they happen to be. However, these are not your kitchen countertop granite slabs. These puppies are four inches thick. They weigh hundreds of pounds and will last a long time. If a slab should break for any reason other than vandalism, the seller should repair or replace it.

You've chosen the stone's color and size. Now you get to choose an inscription, such as "Beloved Mother and Wife," birth date, death date, and graphics such as a mountain scene or the like. This is usually included in the price of the stone as long as the design you choose is from the standard design book you get to browse. If you choose to personalize, it will cost you more. Personalization is a separate design that you want in order for the stone to give more meaning to you and your family. For example, you can, in fact, have Aunt Mildred's portrait cut into the stone. I've done one where an image of the person who had "passed away" (funeral home lingo for families) was etched into the stone on his Harley motorcycle.

My wife and I have prearranged our burial spaces and are stuck with getting a half ledger that will cover half the gravesite. A ledger is a bronze or granite tablet that can cover a fourth, a third, a half, three-fourths, or all of the gravesite. We are getting a standard design of interlocking wedding bands. The inscription will have our names, birth years, death years, and will read "Together Forever".

Should you choose a marker that covers two graves, you will have to pay for another inscription since Aunt Mildred and Uncle Harry will most likely not die on the same day or for that matter the same year. However, should they both die in some fiery car cash or be murdered by their inheritance-minded kids, the final prepaid inscription fee that was in the original contract will either be eaten up by some other unforeseen cost or, least likely, refunded back to your family.

Speaking of markers, should you be of a mind to cremate and scatter your ashes hither and yon, cemeteries have figured a way to make a little profit by providing permanent memorializing. Yes sir, you can buy a letter bar with Aunt Mildred's name, date of birth, and date of death to be placed on a wall somewhere in the cemetery. If you want to go hog wild, you can even buy a grave space and a marker to commemorate a loved one who isn't there. Remember, cemeteries and funeral homes are happy to think of new and different ways to memorialize and honor loved ones because, to them, it's not about the funeral or memorializing, it's about the money.

Bronze flat markers are much the same as the granite markers. Price is dependent on size. They have their own standard graphics you can chose from, and vases can be added. Bronze markers always have to have a concrete or granite base since they are not the four-inch-thick super weights like the granite markers. They take longer to make and deliver and are usually more expensive. They can be made as large as full ledgers and are individually cast. These markers will also need to have a final inscription date cast, so again, there is that additional fee to pay.

Most cemeteries that will accept or require upright markers, or "tombstones," have strict regulations on size, polish, and design. And speaking of designs, make sure you get exactly what you're paying for. After selecting a design for your marker, make sure the standard or personalized design is noted on the contract. The marker will not be made until Aunt Mildred or her spouse dies unless you insist on having the marker delivered to your home, which you can do. But you will still need a final inscription when someone dies. Most people don't have a marker made prior to a death. But I have seen it done. When that happens, the design will be sent to the memorial (marker) maker, and you or your family should receive a proof of the marker to check. If you don't demand and receive a proof, take your business elsewhere because a mistake is forever in the funeral/ cemetery business. Should you sign off on a proof, and there is a mistake, too bad for you. However, if you don't get a chance to sign a proof or the marker comes out different than the proof and a mistake is made, too bad for the cemetery. They have to eat it and make another marker. You may want to prearrange the marker, but personalizations and designs are usually done at the time of death.

You may ask yourself, do I need to get Aunt Mildred a marker? If you don't want one, you don't have to get one. It's nice to have for those that visit Aunt Mildred's grave, but the cemetery can't make you buy one. Moreover, it's illegal for the cemetery to force you to buy a marker. You would be surprised at how many unmarked graves there are. Lastly, if Aunt Mildred is an honorably discharged vet, the Department of Veterans Affairs will provide a flat single-sized granite or bronze marker even if Aunt Mildred won't be buried in a National Memorial Cemetery. That's right; a private cemetery must accept these markers as they must accept any outside marker that meets the cemetery's regulations. Government markers have limited designs, such as a cross or Star of David, and limited personalization. But a government marker doesn't cost the veteran's family. These markers can't be prearranged and can only be ordered at the time of the vet's death.

And then there are flower vases. Oh, yes, you can get a flower vase permanently attached in your stone. Provided the stone is big enough and your pre-need salesperson tells you it's a great addition, the stone will be holed in order to accommodate a vase for flower placement. Or, if the marker is too small, you can buy a separate unit with a vase set in the same granite type and style to be placed about a foot below the stone marker. I wouldn't get either one. There are temporary flower vases sold in garden stores. They are inverted cones that stick into the ground and hold water for your flowers and cost about two to five bucks. Some cemeteries provide temporary flower vases, too. Besides, most cemeteries don't allow artificial flowers and have the right to remove flowers at any time. Usually, flowers and other displays are removed on mowing day. Incidentally, any display, such as pictures, teddy bears, trinkets, balloons, and the like are not allowed. You'll see such displays in cemeteries at any given time, and most cemeteries may tolerate such a display for a period of time, but they have a right to remove such non-regulated items at any time, so don't try to make a home at your loved one's gravesite.

Don't forget the opening and closing of the gravesite you just bought. Yes, they are going to charge you to open (dig the hole) and close (put the dirt back into the hole). However, your salesperson probably will not push this item since many cemeteries will no longer allow you to prepay for the opening and closing, so therefore there is no commission. As you can guess, the opening and closing are only done when someone is actually going to occupy the grave space. It's ninety-eight percent labor and therefore an uncontrollable cost. That labor cost will rise over the years, and the cemetery wants to make a good profit. I've seen prearrangement contracts that were thirty-five years old with the opening and closing charge at fifty dollars. The cemetery must honor that charged service since they took the money for the service even though they will lose money at that price thirty-five years later. Nowadays, opening and closing costs can range from $450 to $1700 or more depending on the cemetery. It's a cost you're family will not be able to get away from, but the good news is that by that time, Aunt Mildred won't care--she will be dead. The cost to the cemetery at the time of this writing is less than $90.

It's unfortunate but a reality; we are all getting bigger. Now, there's big, and there's really big. Gravesites and the merchandise associated with the grave are standardized. The grave liner/burial vault must fit within the thirty-six inch wide allotted grave space. Adult caskets are also standardized in size. So what do you do should the space you just bought be intended for someone greatly obese, say, over three hundred and fifty pounds?

Cemeteries, funeral homes, and casket and burial vault manufacturers, who don't want to limit you to just a cremation and thus leave potential money on the table, have come up with the oversized casket. Yup, this casket is wider, accommodating those who may have grown to five hundred or even six hundred pounds. These caskets cost more than a standard adult size, and, you guessed it, choosing an oversized casket will have other implications.

Since the oversized casket is wider than a standard size, the grave liner or burial vault will also have to be wider, hence, costlier. But it doesn't stop there; because the outer burial container is wider, the gravesite must be wider. However, if a grave space is widened, the cemetery will lose the grave space next to the widened grave because that space will be too narrow for use. Happily for them, the cemetery will have to sell you two spaces for a single interment.

As the customer, you're stuck, but you can negotiate. Your salesperson, who by the way is very pleased with your predicament, should be very amicable about discounting the price of the two spaces. A twenty percent discount on the spaces is very good especially since you're making prearrangements, but always ask for more. Additionally, ask for discounts on the outer container and casket. Your "hammer" is to go somewhere else, and your salesperson knows this even if you don't.

If you choose cremation, you will not need an "oversized" urn; nor will you need two niches, two urn garden spaces, or whatever the case may be (see below). I've never seen or heard of anyone so large that his or her cremated remains did not fit into an adult sized urn.

What if you're prearranging for Aunt Mildred, who's not obese today, but is greatly obese at the time of death? You're going to have to pay the difference; after all, it's not the funeral home or cemetery's fault that your Aunt Mildred ate herself to death. You still may get a discount on the extra grave you have to buy; but, in all likelihood, it won't be a big discount because now that Aunt Mildred has passed away, you're in an at-need situation needing an extra grave space, oversized casket, and grave liner. They pretty much have you over a barrel. One solution, however, is to cremate. If you're the purchaser of the prearranged contract(s) or the representative of the purchaser (Aunt Mildred) and the contract(s) are revocable, then cancel all unnecessary portions of the original contract(s) such as casket and grave liner. Instead of an oversized casket and grave liner, you now have an urn and urn liner. By doing this, you now have *them* over a barrel. If the contract(s) are irrevocable, however, or your family and for that matter Aunt Mildred insist on burial, they have you back over the barrel.

But say you prearranged for an oversized burial, and Aunt Mildred shrunk over the ensuing years and can now fit into a standard-sized casket. The funeral home will apply the cost of the oversized merchandise to the cost of standard-sized merchandise. Don't be expecting a check from the funeral home, though, because in all likelihood the retail cost of the standard-sized casket will be the same if not more than what you paid for the oversized merchandise years ago. If you made the arrangements six months ago, you should get any difference back. The cemetery, however, will not buy back that extra grave you bought for the then obese Aunt Mildred.

Chris R. Bentley

They will happily tell you to use it for someone else; and, by the way, you'll need another marker and outer container for that someone else.

You've got to be done with this new gravesite by now, right? Wrong. Your friendly salesperson will try to hit you up for second rights of interment. These second rights allow you to bury another person in the same spot. How can this be, you ask, if there is already someone in that spot? Well, you can cremate someone and have those cremated remains buried on top of the person already in that spot, or you can put two cremated remains in the gravesite as opposed to a full burial and one urn of cremated remains. I will give more details about cremated remains later. Additionally, some places will restrict the number of second rights of interment in a single space. Where I worked, each grave space was allowed only one second right of interment, thus essentially two burials. Other places allowed up to four rights of interment. I doubt any cemetery would allow twenty cremated remains in one grave space even though I'm sure it could be done. The price for second rights of interment varies, but it's usually a percentage of the price of the gravesite, up to fifty percent; thus, you have now purchased a right to inter, for half the cost, in the same space you just bought. Remember, when you're buying that gravesite, you're only buying one right to inter. And if you do buy second rights, you guessed it—you get to buy even more merchandise, such as another marker, urn liner, etc. Yes, they will sell you up to four markers for a single space, maybe more.

If you don't buy the second rights of interment when you buy the gravesite, the salesperson will threaten you with a price increase for the second rights as the prices of the gravesites in that section of the cemetery go up over time. However, you shouldn't purchase the second rights of interment unless you know absolutely that there is going to be someone using the second right for that gravesite you just purchased. You might be talked into the second-right purchase because you think, "Well, Aunt Mildred's daughter can be cremated and buried with her when her time comes." That might be true; however, chances are that Aunt

41

Mildred's daughter will get married, move across the country, and not want to be cremated and buried with her. The only thing you do know is that she will die someday, somewhere.

Before you leave, the salesperson will play on your emotions because buying a gravesite is an emotional experience, and he will pump you up with enthusiasm for more "stuff" because he knows that buying the extras will, in your mind, blunt the idea of your own death or the death of a loved one. He or she will not want you to forget the lovely bench for your family members to sit on while they contemplate the grass growing over your aunt's dead body. Then there is the sundial, the statuary, and other knick-knacks to brighten your grieving; you came in to buy a grave space, and now you're loaded up with all kinds of merchandise. At the end of this experience, you'll think how understanding the salesperson was, that he gave you a great deal—just what you wanted—when, in fact, you've been had.

Here's the real skinny. If you want a gravesite for full body burial, you *have* to have the following:

1. The gravesite
2. Outer burial container
3. Opening and closing[*]
4. Administration fee[**]

The question of what you should pay is the next consideration. When you are prearranging for cemetery, merchandise, and funeral services, you should never pay the list price. The same does not necessarily hold true for at-need arrangements, but I'll get into that later.

---

[*] Most likely can't be prearranged

[**] Many places will charge an administrative fee. This is around twenty-five dollars for mostly nothing but filing away the contract. You can't negotiate this fee away although it is sometimes waived for at-need cases. Most corporate owned funeral homes charge the administrative fee on pre-arrangement contracts. Many private funeral homes don't.

In perpetual care cemeteries and memorial parks, the price of a grave is broken down into two parts: the grave price and the endowment for care price. The endowment for care portion of the gravesite price is taken from the sale of the grave and deposited into an endowment fund for the perpetual care of the grave. This portion of the gravesite price is usually five percent of the total price. In other words, say the grave is listed at one thousand dollars. The price sheet for that grave should have two numbers: nine-hundred-and-fifty dollars for the grave and fifty dollars for the endowment fund. The endowment-care fund is used by the cemetery for the upkeep of the cemetery. Additionally, when the cemetery is full, and no further sales activities are warranted, the endowment for care fund should be large enough to maintain the cemetery forever.

It's important to know about the endowment for care fund because when you go to buy your grave and you want to get the price down, your salesperson will pull a little trick. Say you want that one thousand dollar grave space, but you want ten percent off the price. Your salesperson will most likely give you that ten percent. However, he will try to limit that ten percent off to the grave portion of the total price. Thus, he reduces the price by ninety-five dollars, not one hundred dollars. He will tell you he can't reduce the endowment portion of the grave space. Just say no; say that you're going to write one check for the space, that you want to spend nine hundred dollars not nine hundred and five dollars, and that you don't care if the cemetery deposits forty-five or fifty dollars into the endowment for care fund. That's their problem, not yours. If you intend to pay for it all at once, you have more leverage. They could make more money over the long run by financing you; however, they want and need your money now. Cash to them is king.

Ten percent is the usual reduction for pre-need buying and is not hard to get. If you're able to manage fifteen percent, you're doing very well. I have heard of up to twenty-five percent off, but that is rare. It's expensive and slow to sell sites, so don't expect them to go that low. Bargaining for price reduction everywhere should be your modus operandi because the markup on everything a funeral home and cemetery sells is huge. One thing I learned from my experiences in the funeral business is that everything every business sells can be bargained. We Americans don't bargain; we see the posted price and pay. I have found that in most buying situations I can tell the salesperson that I think the item is too expensive and ask how much they will reduce the price for me. I usually get a favorable response; and, if I don't, I haven't lost anything.

Other Modes of Interment

Lawn Crypt

An alternative to the side-by-side single gravesites for two would be a double-depth lawn crypt. A double-depth crypt allows for two full-body burials, but takes up the surface area of a single space; they're just much deeper. Cemeteries usually sell these units as packages. With the gravesite, you get the outer container and the marker. Since there are going to be two bodies occupying that three-by-seven-foot space, the outer burial containers have to be built into the space; and when you buy them, the outer container is already set in place. In addition, many cemeteries will allow only one specific style of marker and therefore a packaged price. The advantage to a double-depth lawn crypt is that it is generally more economical than buying two side-by-side spaces and a double-sized marker for the two of you. Plus, there is no outer burial container cost since it's already in the ground. Additionally, this type of interment ownership allows you to buy many second rights, usually two to eight, depending on the cemetery.

This is what my wife and I did. We have an overpriced double-depth lawn crypt with the ability to add second rights of interment for our children if it comes to that. Notice I did not buy the second rights, since the likelihood of one or both of them being cremated and buried with us is low. However, we can purchase the second right if necessary at any time in the future. I also made them remove the price of the marker from the package (they refused to do this until I pointed out that it was illegal to make me buy the marker from them). I could procure the exact same marker for much less through other vendors. There are some advantages to being in the business. Due to the cemetery's regulations, however, I will be forced to buy a half ledger (covering half the gravesite) with the cemetery's restrictions on design and material.

Mausoleums

So Aunt Mildred decides that the thought of rotting in the ground with all that dirt on top of her is terrifying. Instead, she thinks that being desiccated inside a wall is just the ticket. I often wonder why it would matter to anyone how or where their bodies are disposed. I guess it's just a matter of pre-death perceptions. Above-ground burial, or a mausoleum (sometimes referred to as a crypt), has its advantages and disadvantages. Your friendly salesperson is going to give you the same park tour as with the ground burial gravesite except he or she won't be as concerned with selling you a top-end crypt because the cost of any mausoleum is thousands of dollars more than a plot in the ground. Her commission on one single crypt should cover a week's pay or more, and she'll love you for it.

Mausoleums are generally above-ground buildings in which the spaces for the dead are known as crypts. You may purchase single crypts, double crypts, or mausoleums that hold four full bodies. Mausoleums are vented to allow for the escape of gas; therefore, over time, the body will not rot, but dry up like an apricot left in the refrigerator for six months. The great downside to mausoleum burial is the cost. Instead of that nice one thousand dollar three-by-seven-foot plot of ground with the beautiful view of the freeway, it's going to be a four thousand dollar three-by-three-by-seven-foot concrete box usually built in a fashion that protects visitors from the weather. The facings of the crypts are usually covered with a thin layer of marble or granite for aesthetics. Additionally, with few exceptions, you will be required, as a regulation of the cemetery, to be embalmed. The reasoning behind the requirement is that the cemetery doesn't want their mausoleum to smell like a charnel house.

I have known wood caskets in a mausoleum crypt to bulge outward and become wedged in the crypt making disinterment nearly impossible. This is due to gases produced by an unembalmed body expanding in the wood casket. But we'll get to disinterment later.

The price of Aunt Mildred's crypt will depend on location and configuration. If it's a view from on high you're looking for, then choose the top row. They are cheaper. As you go to lower levels the price will increase until you get to eye level and heart level. That would be rows four and three respectively. Row two is less expensive than row three and row one is less than row two. The bottom row (row one) in most modern mausoleums is designed to hold two to four bodies, with the thought that, "The family that's buried together, stays together." Your salesperson will be pitching that sentiment softly and persistently knowing that you'll be thinking of how you can keep the entire family together for eternity.

Crypts are configured in several ways: singles, doubles with caskets laid head to foot, doubles with caskets laid side by side, and foursomes with caskets laid side by side on two separate shelves. All bodies are placed feet first except in side-by-side crypts. The first person who dies in the family will go to the back of the crypt unless of course it's a single crypt. A four-way crypt consists of two levels with the bottom level below the level of the crypt's outer face. The first two bodies occupy the bottom shelf.

Wow! Think of all the second rights you can buy for a four-body crypt. I have heard of one place that sold six second rights of interment for a single-body crypt. For a four-body crypt, you can get your spouse, kids, grandkids, your brother and his family, and the neighbor down the street. There's plenty of room for all those cremation urns and caskets. The only limiting factor is how many names they can get on the front of the family crypt.

However, there are some advantages to purchasing a crypt over ground burial. There is no outer burial container to buy; the crypt itself is the outer burial container. There is no marker per se to buy; however, in order to get the deceased's name in place, you will need to buy what the cemetery requires. Some places will allow a simple "letter bar," which contains the person's name, birth year, and death year. Letter-bar identification is simple, neat, and less expensive than a marker; however, you are less likely to be able to personalize the individual's crypt. Other places allow only a bronze plaque of special size and design, which does allow for more personalization, but it's costly. The cemetery will regulate letter bars or plaques because they want the crypts in the mausoleum to have symmetry and look alike. They may limit the number of second rights just because they don't want eight names on the face of one crypt. Another advantage to mausoleum burial is that the opening and closing costs of a crypt are much lower than those of a grave--no backhoe or dump truck necessary, just two guys, an electric lift, a screw driver, and a chalk gun.

Now, if you really want to throw your money down a rat hole and you've got a hankering to live forever and make a statement to the world that you're rich, buy a private "family" mausoleum. You can find these at older cemeteries where the rich and famous have built monuments to themselves. A private mausoleum can range from a modest above-ground, three-foot-high crypt made of granite, to a walk-in building with a locked gate entrance and shelves for several caskets inside. Either way, you're going to pay a lot of money for one of these puppies. Besides the materials for the crypt itself, you need to buy enough gravesites at the cemetery of your choice to place in the mausoleum. For instance, a two-person, private, above-ground crypt will require four grave spaces, and you have to pay for those spaces. Again, you won't need an outer-burial container; but depending on your personalization of the mausoleum, you could pay mucho bucks.

At one cemetery I know, someone built a private mausoleum attached to the cemetery's public mausoleum crypt offerings, overlooking the ocean. I am told that the individual paid over three million dollars for his monument unto himself. When he and his wife die, I'm sure that his kids would rather inherit the

47

three million dollars instead of pouring the money into a "family crypt," which the kids will not likely use. Remember, a hundred years from now, no one will care unless you're famous.

In some countries, private mausoleums have multiple levels. I've been to Argentina where the crypts go down twenty feet. At each level there are up to eight caskets, room for the whole family and more. However, in nonperpetual care cemeteries (old cemeteries or those in countries such as Argentina), these great eternal monuments to one's family will often fall into disrepair. In some places after so many years of not paying for an individual's family mausoleum upkeep, the caskets are removed and cremated and the space is sold to another family. A friend and mother recently removed their relatives' remains from a mausoleum crypt and stood in line with those remains for cremation along with other families doing the same chore.

I've never sold a private mausoleum in my cemetery selling days. But I know of a potential sale in the cemetery where I worked that was lost through greed. One of our salespeople got an inquiry from a locally famous business owner for a two-person, above-ground, private crypt (mausoleum). Crypts today are pre-made to the customer's specifications, then delivered to the cemetery for assembly. Now our cemetery had never sold and built a private crypt before, but it has always been offered. The sales guy was very excited, as was the sales manager. The potential customer handed over the transaction to his personal assistant who would work out the details with the cemetery.

I knew the salesperson involved, and he was a crook and a liar. The sales manager was not much better, and his deal was to look good at corporate by posting better-than-goal sales figures. These guys were salivating and dreaming of the huge commission they were going to get. The trouble was that the cost of the crypt with property and labor was less than forty thousand dollars. These guys assumed that the buyer's personal assistant was a dummy. And so, they jacked up the price and offered the site and crypt at two hundred and twenty-five thousand dollars. However, the personal assistant was no one's dummy. She did her homework and learned the true cost of the crypt and called the salesperson to tell him no deal. When this idiot of a salesperson tried to renegotiate the price (he offered it at one hundred and fifty thousand dollars), she told him to buzz off and that she was going to find a cemetery she could trust, one that didn't try to rip off her boss. She was mad and had every right to be mad. The two salespeople had lost what would have been a seventy to eighty thousand dollar deal with a commission of over ten thousand dollars.

Urn Placement

Instead of a full-body burial, you've decided that Aunt Mildred's being burned to a cinder is the right thing to do. You want her to be cremated because it's less expensive, ecologically sound, and consistent with her religious beliefs. But at the same time, you want a permanent placement so your loved ones and other curious fellows can view her final, albeit small, resting place. I must say, the ecological reasoning is all bunk. Cremating Aunt Mildred as a way of saving space and the world is just a mindless delusion. There is and always will be grave spaces enough to go around. As long as there is money to be made by selling gravesites, whether ground or mausoleum, there will be space for you and Aunt Mildred. But let's leave that aside for now.

There are many ways to place cremated remains, and the price will depend on the perceived beauty of the urn site or niche. Your salesperson will do the same thing to you as he did with the full-body placement. He'll give you a tour of medium, high, low, and back to medium priced sites. He won't show you the cheapest, which is the common columbarium, also known as the "trash bin," "landfill," and "dumpsite." If the cemetery has one of these sites available, it's something the salesperson doesn't want you to know. But should they have one, you can inquire about that option or find it on their price list somewhere.

The common columbarium is a large container buried in the ground at a remote place within the cemetery. Cremated remains placed in this container are commingled. It is where the cemetery dumps the cremated remains not placed or picked up by families. The cemetery will make an all-out effort to locate a family member and perhaps sell a more "dignified" placement in order to avoid dumping the remains into the columbarium. However, over a period of time, years, they'll give up and dump.

If you choose, you can prearrange for Aunt Mildred's ashes to be commingled at a very low price. Her remains can be dumped on top of someone's Uncle Ernie, who's been abandoned and has languished in some closet for five years at the cemetery then dumped into the common columbarium. No markers or flowers can be placed, and all you can see is probably some cap or plug with a rusty lock to secure the columbarium. As thrifty as I am, even I wouldn't choose this route. But it is available, at a price. I sold this kind of placement once. The guy had no relatives, no one even to scatter his cremated remains, and he didn't care. It cost him fifty bucks at the time.

However, most people think of niches for permanent urn places. Most niches are found in walls, which either stand alone in various places throughout the cemetery, also known as a columbarium, or are found in mausoleums on an outside and/or inside wall. The price you pay will depend on the location of the perceived beauty of the columbarium or niche front you choose. Additionally, niche size can and does dictate urn size. Some niches are made for a certain size and shape of urn. It's a good way of keeping you from buying an urn elsewhere. Should you have a hankering to display that nice urn you bought, most cemeteries have glass-front niches. That's right; you can display the urn, pictures, and some small memorabilia for all to see. You will definitely pay more, but for some people this opportunity to display some items from the deceased's past is too much to give up. Be aware, the cemetery can restrict the items you place in the glass-front niche, including the urn. The cemetery will not allow offensive items or a coffee can as the urn displayed for the public.

Urn Gardens and Ground Placement

Cemeteries will have sections known as urn gardens. This will be an area for urn placement, and due to the shape it would not be suitable for full-body burials. Since cremation is becoming more popular, some places have designed areas with walkways, water features, benches, and appropriate statuary to give it that park-like setting. Of course, the more work they put into an urn garden's aesthetics, the more costly it can be. Where I worked, we had a couple of urn gardens, nothing fancy. They were the least expensive urn placement in the cemetery.

Aside from any aesthetic accoutrements, an urn space in one of those gardens is a grave space as small as one foot by one foot. They're usually sold in packages that consist of the space, marker, and outer burial container. Yes, I said outer burial container. This is just like a full-body burial except smaller. Aunt Mildred's ashes (body) are placed in an urn (casket) and buried, just like your Uncle Joe's full body, with all due ceremony. Of course, the markers are small, and the cemetery will most likely restrict you to one type in order to give symmetry to the entire urn garden.

The outer containers for urns are similar to those for full-body burial. You can arrange for a liner, or you can get an urn vault, which is exactly like burial vaults except they're miniaturized versions. There is an alternative to the traditional outer container—a combination urn and vault. This product is made from very strong and very durable plastic. Most cemeteries accept these combo urn and outer container units, but it's best to check. I found one cemetery that would not accept this type of unit.

You've decided, however, that you don't want Aunt Mildred to be crowded in with all those other people in the urn garden, people you don't even know. However, you want her to be cremated and buried in the ground. Well, your salesperson has a happy alternative for you—buy a full burial plot. Yep, you can buy a full gravesite and have a nice personalized marker and all the associated costs thereof. You get more options for her final resting place, maybe under that nice oak tree. Aunt Mildred's cremated remains will benefit from a less expensive outer-burial container or perhaps the combo urn/outer-burial container depending on your preferences. And the opening and closing fee will be far less than that of a full-body burial. The grounds crew only needs a shovel, not a backhoe. On top of that, you've just made your salesperson much happier because his commission went way up over an urn garden site.

51

Water, Rocks, and a Chair

Many cemeteries, in order to grab more market share, are building alternative urn placements. Besides columbarium (wall), mausoleum, urn gardens, and glass-front niches, now you can be placed under a rock, by a water feature, or in a granite bench.

Wanting Aunt Mildred's cremated remains near water is going to cost more just because she's near water. Sometimes these water features will be a little stream of water meandering through a small section of the cemetery with nice flowerbeds in place and perhaps a bridge or two over the water. Other water features may be a fountain, pond, or waterfall. These are very peaceful settings and very expensive. Along with the water there may be boulders and benches in which to inter Aunt Mildred.

Among the water settings, many places will have urn gardens for ground burial just like in the cemetery but with an up-charge because of the proximity to water. The add-ons are just the same (marker, opening and closing, etc.), but the ground itself is more expensive. Sometimes around the water feature there are boulders. In actuality, these are spots for ground interment. There may be up to six placements of cremated remains around the boulder, but the marker is placed on the bolder itself. This is a very convenient way to up-charge for ground urn interment. Additionally, there will be columbaria or walls in which to place the urns so that they are near or around the water feature. These will be more expensive than columbaria found scattered throughout the rest of the cemetery, and each one will usually be small for a columbarium. Each niche within the columbarium near the water feature is generally built to contain two urns.

How about a nice granite bench? That's right—a bench. The benches are usually already placed around the water feature; however, they are up for sale. The bench allows for much personalization besides names and dates, and they usually hold up to six cremated remains. But, they're costly. You still have to pay for opening and closing. When each person designated to go into the bench dies, there will be a separate final inscription fee in order to put in the date of death. And just because you own the bench, you can't take it with you to a new location, and you can't prevent anyone from sitting on the bench and therefore sitting on your loved ones.

Lastly, if you don't want to be permanently interred in a cemetery, you can prearrange for a cremation and buy your own bench to put in the back yard, or how about at the front porch, or maybe a sundial or boulder in the front yard. You can take cremated remains home if you so choose because as far as the state is concerned the final disposition of the deceased is at the crematory. A cemetery pre-need salesperson will sell you anything for cremation you want or don't want.

Bear some points in mind about any of the burial methods—full body, mausoleum, interment of cremated remains, or take-home interment for cremated remains, in a pre-need arrangement for cemetery spaces and merchandise, your salesperson is most likely on a one hundred percent commission and will up-sell you as much as he can. Let me remind you, the space you pick out will likely have a sharply decreasing visitation by family over time. Therefore, that nice gravesite under the spreading oak may be a waste of money since over time the only one there will be the dead. Merchandise that's being buried is seen only twice—once when it's sold to you and once when it's on display at the funeral or gravesite service.

The hard cold truth is that once Aunt Mildred dies, she won't care. However, her survivors might. Let's be practical. Once dead, the dead do not care if they are buried in the ground or a wall, or cremated and their ashes scattered. The family, however, might want a nice funeral service with all the trimmings and a beautiful view of the valley or mountains. You may also visit a gravesite on a regular basis until you are unable to get to the cemetery. Permanent interment of earthly remains is not necessary. The cheapest and simplest method of body disposition is a direct cremation without ceremony. On the other hand, cemeteries have one thing to offer that may be of interest, and that's permanency. If Aunt Mildred is interred in a cemetery, whether full-body or cremated placement, her family does have a place to go to for remembrance, and it gives her family some sort of history. Pre-need salespeople call this "family heritage." Many times a distant relative is looking for "Uncle Joe" in order to update family history and events, even fifty years after "Uncle Joe" died.

It's all personal preference and what you're willing to spend and put up with. A case in point is a friend of mine and his wife. He doesn't care what happens to him after he dies; therefore, in order to save money, he thinks a direct cremation (box and burn) would be fine. However, his wife has very strong opinions about their interment. She wants a full-body burial for herself because the thought of cremation is horrifying to her. She also wants a full-body burial for her husband. Should he die before his wife, he will be buried in a casket in the ground, something he feels is foolish. And it's not just any cemetery she wants; they're going to be buried in a cemetery close to where they both grew up, a very expensive cemetery. However, his wife's parents and grandparents, and his parents and his grandmothers are all buried at that cemetery. In other words, they have family history there. In order to avoid complaining and a last minute rush to buy cemetery property in case one of them dies suddenly, he acquiesced to her wishes and bought a double-depth lawn crypt. She got what she wanted and some peace of mind, which can be worth the price of dealing with a cemetery lackey, paid a one hundred percent commission. Yet, if he dies after her, he told me he will be cremated because he thinks it's the practical way of disposition.

The best thing about prearrangement is not that you lock down the price fifty years before you die; it's the practicality of having made decisions before a sudden death emergency where you're really going to be vulnerable.

However, in ninety percent of the cases, don't prearrange before you're fifty because you're just throwing away usable cash. There are exceptions however. I remember a couple that came into the combo unit where I worked. They wanted to buy one grave space, a marker, second right of interment, two cremations, two urns, and two outer containers for the urns. He was forty-nine, and she was even younger. Before I took them around the cemetery, I asked why they were prearranging at such an early age; why not wait?

This is not what a salesman should ask since this obviously was an easy sale. The husband's answer was that he was dying. I couldn't believe him. He looked robust and in good health, but I said I was sorry to hear of his impending death. He died six weeks later, and I helped to put his cremated remains into the ground, for him, prearrangement at under fifty, made sense.

Chapter III

Prearranged Funerals

"I want the full-meal deal"

The word *funeral* comes from the Latin *funus*. No, it doesn't mean having *fun* for *us*, but rather to *fade away or die*. Evidence has been found of funeral rites dating back to Neanderthal man with archeological evidence of antler horns and flowers indicating a ritual of remembrance. Many early funeral rites were derived from fear of evil spirits; thus certain rites would rid or placate these spirits. Nowadays there are as many different types of funerals as there are religions.

Okay, it's your funeral. Funerals and funeral services come in all shapes and sizes and can cost a lot of money. There are many things to choose from and decide. Be a shopper and shop hard; but first, get educated. Remember, your prearrangement session is not about the funeral; it's about the money and how your salesperson can get more from you. Always remember, a funeral or memorial service and merchandise is for the living; the dead are gone and don't care.

The funeral itself is simply a ceremony, but there are "funeral" services that are necessary and are usually lumped into a funeral service package. Be aware that there are two sides to the funeral business—handling of the body and disposing of the body. Disposal of a body is generally regarded as the cemetery side except in the case of cremation and no interment. However, handling of the body is considered a funeral service which includes, but is not limited to, picking up the deceased from the place of death, funeral ceremonies, and finally, if the case warrants it, delivery to the cemetery and any services taking place within the cemetery. Until the body is lowered or placed within a niche, you're dealing with funeral personnel.

Remember, we are now talking about the funeral side of the business, not anything to do with the cemetery. Moreover, we are just discussing about prearranging.

Upon inquiry about funeral services and merchandise, the funeral home and staff must provide a general price list. In order to fully understand the nomenclature of a funeral and its associated merchandise, a complete description of the general price list and enumerated charges is warranted.

The General Price List

The general price list is a document that every funeral home in the nation has. Many of the statements on the general price list (GPL) are regulated by the Federal Trade Commission, (FTC). If asked, the funeral home must give you a GPL free of charge. Even a competitor is allowed to ask and receive another funeral home's GPL. *If meeting with a salesperson, that salesperson must give you a GPL before talking about any merchandise or service.* The general price list must have all merchandise and services and the prices listed that the funeral home has to offer. The exception to this rule is that the merchandise price can be given as a range of prices. For instance, the GPL may list a range of prices for caskets, since there are so many to choose from that it would be impractical to list all caskets on the GPL. The funeral home's GPL will show the range of prices and will state something like, "A complete price list will be provided at the funeral home." But even their separate price list for caskets won't have every casket made. The casket price list will reflect the caskets they carry. (Actually, they order these items since they don't want to carry the inventory). Should you want a different casket that is not on their price list, you can be sure they will order it for you and mark it up three to four times over wholesale.

Additionally, you may desire to have certain merchandise not listed but appropriate for the funeral. The funeral home will find and get those items even though they are not on the general price list. Remember, the GPL is only a guide and will only show what they always carry or do as to the services and merchandise. You can choose, pick, and add to those services and merchandise listed.

The cover of a funeral home's general price list is much the same as any other funeral home's. It is required to have the name and address of the funeral home, the phone number, the title "general price list," the effective date, the name of the state and authorizing body that is licensing the funeral home, and the following statement:

"The goods and services shown below are those we can provide to our customers. You may choose only the items you desire. However, any funeral arrangements you choose will include a charge for our basic services. If legal or other requirements mean that you must purchase any items you did not specifically ask for, we will explain in writing on the statement we provide describing the goods and services you selected."

The body of the general price list has categories of services and goods as shown in bold below, with their associated prices or price ranges. In this work, after each category there is a description of the goods or services. All general price lists will have the same categories, but not necessarily the same merchandise or services.

Basic Services of the Funeral Director and Staff

This is a catch-all charge mainly to cover overhead and is added to the cost of your funeral service charges. As I said, sometimes there are packages in which this charge is more than likely included. It softens the blow. This is the charge that covers the cost of all the paperwork, filings, bookkeeping, and time the funeral director spends coordinating all of the above. It is the only charge in the general price list that can't be declined unless you go to another funeral home, which will have the same items on their GPL, but not necessarily the same price.

Use of Equipment and Staff at Another Facility

This charge comprises services outside the funeral home, such as a funeral in a church. It's the meat and potatoes of a funeral director's job. This charge is a big profit center for the funeral home. What this charge means is that they will bring Aunt Mildred to a church or another facility, set things up, such as arranging flowers, handing out folders, and making sure the funeral runs on time and in the right order. This is where the funeral director actually directs the funeral and makes sure the details of the service go off smoothly. It takes a lot of work.

Any surcharges, other charges or add-ons are items such as a memorial service outside the funeral home. The difference between a funeral service and memorial service is the memorial service will not have the remains of the deceased present. If you plan on having a memorial service and you are prearranging Aunt Mildred's funeral, don't buy this item from the funeral home. It's an unnecessary charge; you and your family should arrange Aunt Mildred's own memorial service and it will have more meaning. Should you have questions about what's expected and proper at a memorial service, your funeral director should be happy to help. If he's not helpful, you're in the wrong place.

Other costs in this section of the general price list include overtime charges, particularly for Sundays and holidays. Rosaries, separate prayer sessions, or visitations at a facility other than the funeral home, are all added charges. Do not have any kind of funeral service activity on a Sunday or holiday unless it's for absolute religious reasons that you are not willing to avoid because it's going to cost you plenty.

Use of Facilities and Staff

These charges are almost the same charges you will find under "Use of Equipment and Staff at Another Facility" except you're using the funeral home itself. The charges are usually the same, and you can be sure the funeral home is happy that you are not making them drag Aunt Mildred's body to some church across town. It's pure gravy, and it pays for the empty chapel they have attached to their funeral home.

Other items under this heading are add-ons, such as use of an area of the funeral home for a post-funeral reception and use of a room in the funeral home for visitation, rosary, prayer session, and the like. And, of course, any overtime charges because you insisted on a Sunday or holiday service.

Before we go on, let me say something about visitation. In America, visitation grew out of the necessity to wait a few days before burial in order that family could get to the funeral. Additionally, it allowed people to confirm that the death actually took place. "I don't want to hear that he's dead, I want to see him dead" type of thinking was behind the visitation. Now visitation is hardly needed since everybody can get to a funeral in a relatively short time and should the family allow an open casket funeral, everyone can see "him dead."

So, visitation is now a private family's desire to have their loved ones lie "in state." Instead of the Capitol Rotunda, you're renting a room at the funeral home or elsewhere, and allowing interested friends and family to view the body all day long if they like. My personal feeling is that it's a waste of money, but it's your (or in this case, Aunt Mildred's) funeral.

Preparation of Remains

This section deals with embalming, casketing, dressing of the body, refrigeration, religious washing ceremonies, hairdressing, special care of autopsied remains, and sanitation of unembalmed remains. Many of these charges will most likely end up rolled into a funeral package. But be careful, you might be buying a funeral package and the salesperson might try to slip in something, for instance, "Sanitation of unembalmed remains." It's a bogus charge; don't let the salesperson nickel-and-dime you.

Embalming is the injection of chemicals that delay the deterioration of the cells in the body, while at the same time removing the blood from the vascular system. Embalming is an art. Too much or too little embalming fluid will make the deceased, grey, white, or yellow. States now have laws and regulations about embalming and how long an unembalmed corpse can be out in the open environment. Generally, six hours is the limit to have an unembalmed body out of refrigeration, and you really don't want more. Therefore, if you are going to have a viewing /visitation or an open casket funeral, embalm. However, if, after your aunt dies, no one will be looking in on her and your plans are to just head on up to the cemetery, you don't need to be embalmed. If she is being entombed in a crypt, the cemetery will probably require embalming, as explained above.

All general price lists will say that embalming is not required by law except under certain circumstances (crypt burials and cross-country trips). If you don't want embalming, you don't have to pay for it. If fact, the only way I know of that a funeral home can force you to embalm is if that funeral home has no way of keeping the body cool. I've heard of it, but it's very rare. There is no evidence of unembalmed bodies causing disease from a cemetery. I've even heard the line that unembalmed bodies can be a danger to groundwater. Should your salesperson give you a song and dance about sanitizing and disinfecting, you're being handed a load of crap, and he's trying to play to your sense of community and guilt. Don't buy it; embalming is useful for one purpose and one purpose only: cosmetics. If you're going to have viewings and open caskets, by all means embalm; but don't embalm for the wrong reasons, namely because your salesperson wants you to.

If Aunt Mildred is to be embalmed, you won't get a refrigeration charge. On the other hand, if she doesn't get embalmed you still probably won't get a refrigeration charge. All bodies are refrigerated upon delivery to the funeral home. In most cases the refrigeration charge is waived since in most cases you're going to pick out a funeral service package that includes refrigeration and the body will be disposed of within three or four days. However, should you or your family delay the disposition of the body (you're waiting for Aunt Gertrude to get to town or fighting amongst yourselves over the funeral arrangements), the funeral home should and will nail you for this charge. By the way, the charge for embalming and the charge for refrigeration are usually the same.

Other charges under this category include dressing and cosmetics, religious washing (the family does the work, but the funeral home charges; it's justified since a funeral director must be present), casketing (usually not charged should you buy the casket from the funeral home, but you'll get charged if you buy the casket from somewhere else), hairdressing (justified if needed), sanitation of unembalmed remains (sometimes but not always justified), and special care of autopsied remains. The last item is very justified because it is nasty work and takes some skill. Don't expect the funeral home to discount these items. There is a lot of labor involved and not much profit. Even the high-priced funeral homes don't make their bread and butter in preparation of remains. This doesn't mean you can't ask for a little discount, but don't expect it. Of course, if your funeral services are going to consist of cremation, preparation of remains becomes a mute point.

Transportation

If it moves, charge it. That's right, anytime the funeral home has to move a body or anything else, they will charge you. Transportation of the deceased from the place of death is usually a flat fee provided you died within twenty-five or thirty miles of the funeral home. Any extra mileage for the transportation of anything will come with an additional mileage charge, usually about a dollar and fifty cents to three dollars per mile over the funeral home's stated limit. These extra charges are on the GPL. Other charges may include utility vehicle or flower car (it's just a van, nothing special), transportation to the airport for those of you being buried somewhere else, and limousines for the grieving family. Limousines are usually rented from a limousine service and up-charged. You can arrange for the limo service yourself; you might save a few bucks. There are transfer charges to the crematory or to a place for autopsy. The funeral home can even charge you hundreds of dollars for the short hearse ride (now called a coach) from their own chapel to the burial site within their own combo unit. But they usually won't, since it will be in a package deal.

It's hard to get a discount on any of these charges; however, you probably won't pay for them separately. These charges are usually buried in a package deal. For instance, say you are arranging for a graveside service and burial. The cost of the coach to bring the deceased to the graveside service should not be an add-on if you're dealing with a combo unit and you're burying within their cemetery. Instead it should be included with the cost of the graveside service. If the funeral home tries to add this cost on, use someone else. On the other hand, if you are dealing with an independent funeral home that doesn't have its own cemetery or the funeral home has a cemetery but you're burying somewhere else, expect to pay for the coach to get the body to the place of burial.

Merchandise

This is a gravy maker for the funeral home. On the general price list, things like caskets, outer burial containers, and urns are listed with a price range since there are too many choices. The GPL will state that a complete price list for such items will be provided upon request. When you are considering such items, the general practice is to not show you the lowest cost items on the price list. In many cases, there won't be even a picture of the lowest cost item. Remember, you're prearranging a funeral and all its trimmings.

The funeral home will have on display items that they want to push. But if an item doesn't sell, they will not display it.

Market influences play a part in displayed items. Many items that are purchased are ordered by the mortuary to avoid carrying Inventory. For example, the funeral home has the casket you want on display, but that particular casket is not the one you get. The ordered casket will come from the vendor, usually overnight. Some funeral homes won't even have caskets on display; but will have small butt ends of caskets mounted on the wall. Additionally, the funeral home will have on hand several catalogues of merchandise for you to look through upon request. Most of those catalogues will not be in the same room where you're planning your funeral, because the salesperson doesn't want to overwhelm you with choices (and take up too much of his time). But if you don't see what you like or had in mind, ask to see more catalogues of the item(s) you're deciding on. After all, it's your money and funeral, not the salesperson's.

Special Charges or Other Services

This part of the GPL deals with low-end services that are packaged. Usually, these services consist of "Forwarding of Remains to Another Funeral Home," "Receiving Remains from Another Funeral Home," "Direct Burial," and "Direct Cremations." This section can also contain up-charges for obese cases and/or charges for unspecified services.

Forwarding of Remains to Another Funeral Home

Say Aunt Mildred retired in Las Vegas, but she wants to have services in her old hometown in Nebraska where her family has been buried there for the last two hundred years. All she wants is to get to her funeral on time, but how. The forwarding of remains accomplishes just that—death in one place, services and burial in another place. The price will include transfer from place of death to the funeral home; body preparation, such as embalming; refrigeration; and transfer to a common carrier, most likely an airline. The price will not include a casket or an air tray, which has a plywood bottom and cardboard top box in which to place the casket during shipping. The air tray is required by the airlines and will protect the casket from damage. The price will not include any other services or items you may desire. Should your aunt want to have a funeral service at her new home plus one at the town of burial, it's going to cost.

For forwarding to another funeral home, embalming will be necessary, except in cases where religion forbids embalming. In those cases, the remains will be placed in a special casket commonly known as a Ziegler, which is a sealed, zinc-lined metal box. Upon arrival at the receiving funeral home, she is either transferred into a more traditional casket (if you want to pay for another casket), or just buried in the Ziegler.

Receiving Remains from Another Funeral Home

This is a package where the receiving funeral home will pick up the remains from the nearest practical airport, transfer them to the funeral home for services, or just transfer the remains to the cemetery for burial. If you have a service at the receiving funeral home, you will be charged more than just the package of "receiving remains." In many instances, people retire and die somewhere, but want to be buried in the family plot in their old hometown. However, nobody in the old hometown remembers "Uncle Joe" so there is no need for a funeral service.

In both cases of "forwarding remains" and "receiving remains," you have to make arrangements with two separate funeral homes. If you are arranging for the shipping of remains, a good funeral home will help you with dealing with the funeral home you are either shipping to or receiving from. At my funeral home, we not only found a funeral home on the receiving or shipping end, we also shopped it. We always got three "bids" and checked the Internet to see if there were any posted complaints about the funeral home we were going to recommend to our client. However, it is always the client's responsibility to choose the funeral homes on each end.

The above also applies in cases of death overseas. You will need both "forwarding" and "receiving" funeral homes. The funeral directors in both countries will have more paperwork to fill out (try getting a body out of Bulgaria), but the principles are the same.

Immediate Burial

OK, so Aunt Mildred has a gravesite, but doesn't want any services after she dies. This is the deal for her. The "immediate burial" section will have a price range, which will consist of a choice of buying a casket from the funeral home or you providing your own casket. In other words, there's the "immediate burial" cost and the cost of a casket, never mind the cemetery costs. An "immediate" or "direct" burial will get you transportation from the place of death, refrigeration, basic services of the director and staff (the paperwork), and delivery to the hole in the ground.

Immediate burials take place at the cemetery's discretion since there is no related service and therefore no mourners to attend the burial. You can't add services on to this package since adding on service(s) would make it not an immediate burial.

The "immediate burial" won't get you a casket, outer burial container, marker, or the opening and closing. Such merchandise and services are cemetery items that you will have to buy or have already arranged. But it's a cheap way to get your aunt to the boneyard.

Direct Cremation

The "direct cremation," sometimes known as the "box and burn," is becoming more and more popular. Why? Because it costs far less than a full-body burial. In this category, you will again find a price range: from the price of the "direct cremation" to the price of the "direct cremation with a cremation casket or container." In most places that I know of, a body must be placed in a rigid container before it's placed in the crematorium; it's the law. Therefore, you have a choice of cremation containers of which the "alternate container" is the most popular since it costs less.

Cremation caskets are a waste of money unless you're having a funeral service before the cremation; but we'll get into that later. Besides, you can't add services to a direct cremation. Needless to say, to buy a nice cherrywood casket and then burn it is a sinful waste of money and wood. Choose the alternate container, which is just a seven-foot long cardboard box. Many places will have the alternate container rolled into their basic package, but the Federal Trade Commission (FTC) requires them to split it out on the general price list. Hence, the two prices of "direct cremation" and "direct cremation with a cremation casket or container." Remember, you don't have to buy any item from the funeral home except the basic services of the director.

Additional Service and Merchandise or Cash-Advanced Items

This is a list of merchandise and services whose costs can't be guaranteed if you are prearranging. For instance, say you want a certain flower arrangement at your Aunt Mildred's future funeral service. You've looked through the catalogue and find that the arrangement costs two hundred dollars, but she lives for another fifteen years. The funeral home is not going to risk that the flower arrangement you picked out is going to cost two hundred dollars next year, much less in fifteen years. So, you put down two hundred dollars for the flowers and she lasts another fifteen years, at which time those flowers cost three hundred and fifty dollars. Someone's going to have to pony up the additional one hundred and fifty dollars, or there will be no flowers.

Other non-guaranteed items might include but not be limited to death certificates, other filing fees, motorcycle escorts, limousines, memorial folders, and the like. As I said before, these are items that the funeral home has no control over and are subject to their vendors' whims. I can guarantee that the price

67

you see on the general price list, or any other price list, has been marked up *except for items such as death certificates and other government filing fees*.

That's the general price list. Certain phraseology, as well as the price list's format, are required by the FTC. It will not tell you that you can buy any of the services or merchandise from whomever you want. The funeral home will assume that you don't know that you can buy a funeral service from them and the casket from someone else. But now you know and knowledge is power.

So, let's review the basics for prearrangement of funeral services. The following list of basics are not to be confused with packages where such basic services are usually included in a package.

What you need for full-body funeral/burial are the following:

1. Basic services of the director and staff
2. Transportation
3. Refrigeration and/or embalming
4. The funeral service, if desired
5. Casket
6. A death certificate and any required state/county filing fees

The cemetery costs, as explained above, are separate.

Full-body Funerals

Say your father is getting on in years and you have decided that it's time to plan the final act in his life. You desire a full-body burial at the local cemetery and have made those cemetery arrangements, but now you have to go to your favorite funeral home to plan the end game. Because your father has some stature in the community and lots of friends and relatives, you have decided that a funeral service would be better than dropping him off at the funeral home, opening his will, cashing the check, and forgetting about him.

The salesman is delighted that you've chosen a funeral service as opposed to a "box and drop." If you just walk in without an appointment, the pre-need salesperson on duty will be wetting his pants at his good luck. And he's really going to help you—help you lighten your wallet.

You'll be brought into a "family arrangement" room where your eyes will take in a myriad of merchandise. The salesperson will bring in catalogues, contracts, notepaper, and an empty file folder. The first thing he'll want is your name, phone number, and the name of person the arrangement is for. He will take note of your dress, watch, and perceived education level, trying to get a handle on your financial status.

After some general banter and questions about your father, it's time to get down to brass tacks. Your salesman will start talking about memorializing and honoring your father. In other words, spending more money. This will be done while the salesperson is gathering vital statistics (death certificate information). Although vital statistical information is needed when the death certificate is being produced, it also gives the salesperson an idea of the economic status of your family. Incidentally, when your father dies, the funeral director is going to go over the vital statistics again anyway.

The salesperson will probably suggest you buy a funeral package deal, and buying a packaged deal might be the smart thing to do. These packages are designed to sell you more than what you want, but make you feel good about the purchase. The packages generally will include basic services of the director and staff, transportation of the deceased to the funeral home, refrigeration/embalming, the funeral service, a viewing, the coach, flower van, and maybe some extras like a death certificate. Most packages offered will have in common the necessary services for the care and disposition of the decedent. The difference between packages is the amount of "fluff" in each package. And if you compare the price of a funeral package deal

69

item for item against the general price list, you will find a better deal going with the funeral package.

Remember, however, what the salesperson's motivation is: getting you to buy more. He's going to do that by hammering the memorializing and honoring theme and provoking a little guilt to get you to go for a more expensive package or expand the package with extras. But in my opinion, memorializing and honoring are extremely personal. The salesperson, while showing sympathy and understanding, actually doesn't give a rip about your father; he just wants to build up his commission and post-sales. On top of that, your salesperson won't even be involved with the funeral service because he's not a funeral director, even if your father falls dead the day after you sign and pay the contract. He won't give a rat's rear end.

Your problem will be an emotional control problem. You might even think that you are arranging your loved one's services with the detachment of a bank loan officer; after all, you are planning this before his death with a clear and objective eye, aren't you? But in the back of your mind, even subconsciously, you're thinking "he's my father, my loved one—he deserves these things, and he deserves to be memorialized and honored." And the staff at the funeral home knows what you are thinking. If your father was, in fact, dead already, they could throw in guilt to help you lose your money. Remember, it's not about the funeral; it's about you and your money.

Now let's go through your arrangements for your father item by item for a typical funeral. I'm going to put down some price ranges for each item, and you'll see how shopping is important. These prices will vary depending on what part of the country you're in and the funeral home you've picked; if costs are higher or lower in your part of the country, the above is still relevant to this discussion.

Say you've chosen a funeral home. The very first charge is for "basic services of the director and staff," anywhere from $750 to $2500. Since the funeral director from your funeral home will be directing and supervising all the paperwork and services you desire, you cannot say, "No, I don't want this service"; but you can negotiate the price. Everything else you can refuse and/or buy somewhere else if desired.

Next you have transportation charges for picking up your father from the place of death (usually within thirty miles of the funeral home), about $150 to $400. Included with transportation (but at an extra charge), will be the flower or utility vehicle at $175 to $250, coach (hearse) at $250 to $400, limousines at $250 to $400 each, and escorts at $125 to $300 each. You will need to pay for the pick up of the deceased (sometimes known as the first call); and if you have any flowers at the funeral service, they're going to get you for the flower car. The coach is necessary for transportation to the cemetery unless there is no graveside service; in that case, they should transport to the cemetery by the utility vehicle at either a lower cost or no cost. Don't get limos for your family unless you absolutely can't drive to the cemetery for the interment. And don't drive to the cemetery in "procession" otherwise, you will have to have escorts. Let all the people coming to the graveside service get there on their own.

Refrigeration usually comes with any package you choose, even a direct cremation package. Your loved one will be refrigerated upon pick up no matter what. However, should you decide not to go with a packaged deal, some places will charge you refrigeration fees. Additionally, should you not inter or cremate the body in a reasonable amount of time, the funeral home will start charging a daily refrigeration fee. Refrigeration fees can be negotiated (that cooler is on all the time no matter how many bodies are occupying it). Funeral homes tend to be easy about such fees.

Embalming has been around since the early Egyptians, but was not popular in the United States until the Civil War. It was virtually impossible to get fallen loved ones from the battlefield to their homes for proper burial during the war because of distances and time. However, several surgeons started to embalm fallen soldiers, charging their families seven to twenty-five dollars in order that the battlefield dead could be shipped home without decomposing. Dr. Thomas Holmes became known as the "father of modern embalming," having embalmed about four thousand officers and men. Embalming popularity really skyrocketed when Abraham Lincoln became the first U.S. president to be embalmed (by guess who? Dr. Holmes). Because Lincoln was embalmed, he could lie in state for days and then take a two-week trip to Illinois without smelling like last week's fish catch on a hot afternoon.

Don't embalm unless you need to. Embalming does slow down decomposition; thus, it "preserves" a corpse for a reasonable time. If, however, you're not having a visitation or a funeral service with an open casket or being interred within a mausoleum, don't waste your money. Many funeral service packages will include embalming. Embalming is not only a science; it's an art form. Don't be surprised that your father is a little too yellow or he's hard as stone; not all embalmers are good embalmers. On the other hand, if you're going to show the body at visitation or at the funeral, embalm just for cosmetic reasons. Death isn't pretty and as time goes on, it gets uglier. A good embalmer doesn't want your father to look the same as when he was thirty-five; what he wants to do is take away the ravages of the disease or injury he suffered before he died, to make him look at rest but not necessarily perfect. Once, we had a person who was to have an open-casket funeral, but the family didn't want embalming. In spite of four days of refrigeration and nearly two hours applying cosmetics, the deceased never looked quite right.

The funeral service is the big daddy. But what it really means to the funeral home is that the funeral director will now earn his money by coordinating an event. If you look on a general price list you will notice that for most funeral homes, a funeral service at the funeral home or at a place of your choosing is the same price. Should you have a funeral at a church, the church may charge the funeral home, which will in turn pass the fee, or even add more, on to you. That's why the price for a funeral, whether on-site or off-site, is the same. They want you to use their funeral home's chapel so you avoid additional facility charges; it's easier for the funeral home and justifies the cost of maintaining the chapel. The coach charge makes up for dragging your father across town when having the service at an outside facility.

That being said, the funeral director will coordinate services such as the music, handing out memorial folders, arranging the flowers, acquiring and contacting clergy, and all the little things needed and wanted. The service will have order to it, such as when the eulogy is given or whether friends and family will be allowed to say something about the dearly departed. This is the director's job, but it's your job to pay for all the extras. Therefore, the funeral service doesn't mean you get the clergy, music, flowers, memorial book, etc.; it means you get someone to coordinate all of the above and schedule a time and place for all to happen. Any of these extras are solely at the discretion of the purchaser, not the salesperson.

If you plan to bury and have the funeral in a combo unit, there should be no charge for transportation from the funeral home to the gravesite. After all, the gravesite is probably less than a quarter of a mile away. If the funeral home wants to charge you for a coach and utility vehicle for this little trip, tell them no. Transportation to the funeral home's own cemetery is usually rolled into a funeral package. Otherwise, threaten to take your business elsewhere. The funeral home will buckle under. On the other hand, if the funeral is off-site, expect to pay for these two vehicles, but negotiate the price.

Lastly, if you have a full funeral and wish to have a gravesite service immediately following, you shouldn't pay for both. If the funeral home won't perform a gravesite service or interment after the chapel service free, you're at the wrong funeral home.

Next, you'll be asked to pick out a suitable casket for your ailing father. What I mean by suitable is what the salesperson can get out of you in order to "honor and memorialize" your dad. Caskets come in two forms—wood and metal. Here again, the salesperson is going to show you the medium, then high, then low, then back to medium priced products. Wood caskets go from plain plywood boxes to fir, oak, pecan, cherry, and highly polished mahogany; and the price will depend on which wood you pick. Some will have keepsake drawers built into the lid for the placement of items and notes you want buried with your father.

Then you have the metal caskets. These come in all types and colors. I will go from cheaper to idiotic in price. First, there are the mild steel caskets, which come in several colors and gauges. Gauges are the measurement of the thickness of the steel, for instance a twenty-gauge steel casket is made of mild steel, meaning that if twenty sheets of such steel are stacked together, the stack would measure one inch. Needless to say, the lower the gauge of steel, the thicker the casket and more expensive. The cheaper steel caskets will not seal when closed, and there is no gasket for the casket, not that it really means anything. For a little more money, you can get a mild steel casket with a "mono-seal" gasket. So what?

Next, there is the stainless steel casket; yup, you bet, made out of stainless steel. The sales pitch: won't rust, looks nice. So what? A grade up is the copper casket; sales pitch: it's copper, won't rust, looks nice. So what? Then there's the bronze casket; sales pitch: won't rust, won't turn green like a copper casket, and looks nice. So what? If your salesperson is good, he or she will present you with a variety of casket corner caps. Corner caps fit on the corners of caskets and have nature, military, or religious themes. Likewise, in the interior of the casket, you can have an embroidered head panel. A head panel is a cloth-covered panel that fits inside the lid of a casket directly above the head of the deceased with themes similar to those on the corner caps. All of these are designed to enhance your casket buying experience and relieve you of your hard-earned money. But for some, these items do enhance the memory of the event.

Should your salesperson go on about the comfort of the interior of the casket, you know you're being up-sold. Your deceased loved one will not care about or know the difference. In other words, don't upgrade for comfort. Get the casket you like and can afford.

Why am I so sarcastic about caskets, you might ask? Well, because no one cares. The casket will be on display for the visitation, the funeral service, and the gravesite service. Now you see it, now you don't. There's no need to spend a lot of money on a box that will be buried or put into a wall and most likely not be seen again. Sure, at a funeral with family and friends you may not want your father laid out in front of everyone in a plywood box. But you don't need to spend twenty-five thousand dollars on a thing that looks like a space pod out of the movies, then put six feet of dirt on top of it in a few hours. (Yes, there are twenty-five thousand dollar caskets.)

I once sold two copper caskets to a representative of a woman whose husband had already been interred at the cemetery where I worked. The agent's mission was to pre-arrange for the lady's ship-in (receiving remains from another funeral home) and burial in our mausoleum. There was a twist, that is, there was no space next to the already deceased husband, so I had to sell two new mausoleum spaces, buy back the space the husband was in, arrange for a disinterment (more on that later), and sell two new ones since she wanted matching caskets.

The woman's personal representative (she had no other family) had carte blanche and didn't care how much any of this was going to cost. So, when we got around to picking out caskets, he fell in love with the copper casket we had on display. I pointed out to him that there was absolutely no reason for such an expensive casket since no one would be present at the interment of this woman. He didn't care. He said that the casket suited her and that's what she was going to get. I also told him that the husband was already in a casket, so why buy a new one for him? He told me that the husband was in a wood casket and that the woman wanted something nicer for the both of them.

When she died, we sent someone five hundred miles round trip (and charged for those miles), disinterred the husband, put her and her husband in the new caskets, threw out the old casket (it's illegal to resell a used casket), charged for casketing husband and wife, and put them into their new digs together. What a waste of money, and the representative didn't care because it wasn't his money; he had no dog in the fight.

Here's a word about buying your casket from places other than the funeral home, the likes of Costco, the Internet, or other such places. It is your right to shop and buy from any source you choose. But, unless you plan on taking that casket home and storing it in your garage, don't do it. Caskets are a one-time, immediate-use item. If you're prearranging, but want to buy from a source other than a funeral home, be afraid. You might get a great deal from, say, Costco, and they will hold that casket until needed. But, when you do need it, it gets sent to the funeral and if it is damaged, you can't take it back to your nearest Costco and expect to get a replacement in time. Additionally, make sure the casket will fit into the space allotted. An upscale retail store had handmade caskets from Africa in their catalogue. Trouble was that none that I saw would fit into an outer burial container or mausoleum space.

The funeral home will take no responsibility for any damaged casket that they did not order themselves. In one case, a Mormon family decided to bypass the funeral home, purchasing a casket for their father from the Internet. It was good that they shopped and they saved some money. However, what arrived at the funeral home before the service was not what they wanted. The casket this family received was designed to accommodate a Catholic woman. The family was unaware of the problem until they arrived at the chapel and got a look at Dad resting peacefully in his nice pink casket.

Needless to say, the family became unglued. With no way to return the casket or replace it in time, the service went on as scheduled. The family gazed upon this casket with its array of saints, crosses, and the Virgin Mary during the service and again during the gravesite interment service. I understood the family's angst, but look on the bright side. Once the box is dropped and the dirt is dumped, no one will ever see it again. But they still have their memories!

The moral of the story is to buy your funeral merchandise from a funeral home, which can then be held responsible for any damaged or missing ordered items. You can even arrange for funeral services at one funeral home while buying funeral merchandise at another funeral home. Therefore, if anything is wrong at the last minute, the item can be replaced fast; and you have someone to talk to directly who's accountable.

Finally, you get to the last items in the prearrangement of your father's funeral—death certificates and state and/or county filing fees. Some funeral packages will include one death certificate and maybe the filing fees. These items are pass-through costs that the funeral home doesn't make any money on. If the funeral home is tacking on a fee to process, pay, and obtain these fees and death certificates, get out; use someone else. The number of death certificates you will need will be dependent on the size and complexity of the deceased's estate. You can always get more from your funeral home or the county in which the person died, so don't go hog wild unless you need to.

That's it; flowers, memorial cards, memorial books, clergy, and pictures don't need to be prearranged since the funeral home can't guarantee their future cost. If you want such items, save your money until the final arrangements at the time of death.

If you just want a graveside service, it should be cheaper. Be aware of packages that will sell services and items and give you a choice, for example, a package for all services with a choice of a funeral service, a memorial service, or a gravesite service and for only fifty-seven hundred dollars. Well, the graveside service should be cheaper; it's cheaper for the funeral home to do because there is not so much planning and no building use. Negotiate the price, always negotiate the price. If you threaten to go somewhere else, they'll cave.

When presented with a package deal, unravel the items listed in the package, compare those items with the same items on the general price list. The price should be higher than the package deal. However, eliminating some of the items in the package deal may in turn get you below the package price. For instance, you may not want a day of visitation. Look on the general price list and tell the salesperson that you'll take such and such package, but you want the three hundred dollar visitation cost removed from the cost of the package. The salesperson will tell you that the package is the package and take it or leave it. You tell the

77

salesperson to ask his manager about reducing the price. Nine times out of ten they'll eliminate the sum or a portion thereof from the package price.

Okay, so you're looking at a package deal for funeral services; but you're thinking, I don't want to see my father laid out in a casket and I certainly don't want to be at the graveside and watch him be lowered. What about the memorial service choice? Usually this is not a good choice. Memorial services are funeral services without the body or cremated remains. Families will hold a memorial service for someone who is missing but in all likelihood dead. Therefore, you don't need a funeral director, unless you want to pay him or her a lot of money to pass out memorial folders. You can have the funeral home find a site for the service and prepare things like memorial folders, but you don't need the director, which is what you're paying for. Some families will have a simple private funeral and/or graveside service, then a public memorial service not involving the funeral home. If you're going to do a memorial service, do it yourself. That way it's much easier to plan. There's no time crunch, and you can have it where and when you want. It can be very personalized with music and pictures, for example. I know of memorial services held at churches, parks, ocean beaches, homes, restaurants, and even bars. Again, you don't need a funeral director.

Remember, the salesperson is going to hammer you with the memorializing and honoring line, which is designed to make you feel guilty for short sheeting your poor old father. Get what you want, not what the salesperson tells you what you need to make things look good. You're the one who knows how to honor and memorialize your father, not the salesperson. Think carefully. Do you want the funeral home to provide a reception area after the service or would you rather have the reception at your home? You'll pay for theirs, but not for yours. For every piece of merchandise you will buy, there is a more expensive one or less expensive one. For instance, maybe you like mahogany wood or your father loved to work with mahogany. So, you think that a mahogany casket would be "honoring" your father. But mahogany caskets are expensive. Think about getting something less expensive, yet good looking, such as walnut. It will cost you less, and you know what? Your father will never *see* it anyway. For you, it's a matter of what you desire and should not be based on guilt. Balance what you want against what it costs; is it really worth the money in the long term?

Prearrange your father's funeral to be as grand or simple as you want. Don't be bludgeoned into buying services and items that in the long run don't mean anything. The guilt trip is an expensive trip. Once you've decided on your father's funeral, you'll get a second chance to review and modify the arrangements upon your father's death. Yup, even though you have made all these arrangements beforehand, you have to come in and review, schedule, sign authorization papers, sign interment papers, and possibly modify the plan should you so desire. And they get a second chance at you. Only this time you'll be seeing a funeral director or assistant director and possibly a salesperson whose job it is to finalize the cemetery arrangements and sell more or upgraded merchandise.

Cremations

Ah, cremation, the funeral home's nightmare, yet it could be their bread and butter. Unfortunately for the funeral homes, more and more people are choosing cremation because it's less expensive (usually), and simpler, and some people are concerned about the environment and land space. (The last reason is bogus, but people have preconceived misconceptions). At the National Association of Funeral Directors' 2008 convention, most seminars were how to increase revenue through cremation packages. The answer was to promote the fluff in order to make up for the revenue shortfall that simple cremations don't generate. One owner stated that he won't do a direct cremation for under three thousand five hundred dollars , and he's getting an average of four thousand five hundred dollars per cremation case. How does he do it one may wonder? Simple: a) his clients don't know that the funeral home down the street may offer the same services and merchandise at a much fairer price, in other words the client thinks this price is the norm, b) the client doesn't care that he's being hosed, or c) the client feels guilty not getting the very best for his loved one.

Cremations run from a simple direct cremation, otherwise known as the "box and burn," to an elaborate funerals then off to the crematorium. I've done them all. Again, this is a funeral home service, and we will not include cemetery services and merchandise in this section. So, let's go over some of the ways you or yours could be cremated. For those that don't know, you might be very surprised at what can be done and how fast the bill increases.

What you need for cremation is the following:

1. Basic services of the director and staff
2. Transportation
3. Refrigeration
4. The cremation process with container
5. The death certificate and any required state/county filing fees

However, the above list is a little misleading because if you wanted a simple direct cremation, but paid the above items individually from the funeral home's general price list, you would be paying too much. Of course, a simple "direct cremation" is in the general price list containing the above items, except possibly number five, bundled into a lower-priced package.

The above being said, you should be familiar with the packaged cremation deals. Packaged cremation deals are much like full-body funeral deals—rolled-up services and merchandise offered at a lower price than when individually chosen from the general price list. Cremations are a problem for funeral homes, especially large corporate-held homes. Why? Because a direct cremation doesn't cover the funeral home's bloated overhead. However, a good salesperson will focus on the memorializing and honoring guilt trip and try to get you to add a service or at least a nice cremation casket. After all, doesn't your father deserve the very best?

My personal favorite deal is the "direct cremation." It's the least costly, provides everything needed for disposition by law, and is the least complicated arrangement in the funeral industry. Should you choose direct cremation, when all is done, the funeral home will give you her remains (ashes) in a plastic bag contained within a cardboard box. If you choose to "box and burn," you can pick Aunt Mildred up in three or four days, bring her home, and she's sitting on the mantle place for all to see.

If you like, you may add an urn, which in my opinion is nicer than a cardboard box for you and your relatives to gaze upon. However, you don't have to buy the urn from the funeral home. You could go to a store like Pier One Imports, as I did with my dog, and find something appropriate. It's your choice. Another choice is to scatter her remains to the four winds. If you scatter, don't buy an urn—you don't need one. Funeral homes will even sell what is known as a scattering urn which is made for the scattering of cremains, and you get to keep the urn as a keepsake. It's a waste of money. I have never sold a scattering urn because I have never let my clients buy one.

Another option is the portioning urn or miniature urn. Some families will scatter, but want to keep a small portion of their dad as a memento. The difference between a portioning urn and miniature urn is the size. The portioning urn will hold more of him. I once sold ten urns to a family whose mother had passed away--one full-sized urn, containing half of her cremains for Dad, and nine miniatures for the children, nieces, and nephews. They all wanted a piece of Mom.

My second favorite cremation deal is a direct cremation, but you supply the memorial service. The funeral home would love to do the memorial service because they have to do nothing except schedule the place and time. Save yourself some money and find your own place. The funeral home can help if need be. Have the funeral home make the memorial cards and supply the memorial book, but keep them out of the memorial service itself. Remember, for everything they have to do, you pay.

There are other things you can add to a direct cremation package. One that is popular is the "identification viewing."

This is where you're at the funeral home and you want to see Dad before the big burn, but you don't want an all day visitation. Most identification viewings are made right after you make all the final arrangements. Before you leave, you get to see your dearly departed. The funeral home will pull the deceased out of refrigeration, place him on a rolling stainless steel table, cover him with a blanket, maybe put a pillow under his head, perhaps clean up the face a little, and possibly comb his hair. Should you have an identification viewing and the body is presented to you in the original plastic bag without being covered and no attempt made to improve his appearance, you should be outraged. Throwing a body in a plastic bag on a table for family to view, without any attempt to soften the situation, doesn't show respect for the deceased, and it shows disrespect for you, their customer. To show you a body as they have found it demonstrates that they don't care about you or the deceased; they just want you gone and your check in hand. You most likely will be charged for this added extra, but some places will do it free. Most of the time my funeral home did it without charge even though the funeral home was not located where we kept our "clients." Remember, they have to do something, namely retrieve the body from the refrigerator; put it on a table; do a little prep work; and then, when all is said and done, put the body back.

Then there's the witnessed cremation. That's right, a direct cremation that you, the family, can witness. What you get is a body in a box, which is then placed inside the retort (that's the crematorium apparatus); if you're lucky, you get to push the start button. Funeral homes will charge you for this privilege since it must be scheduled and a funeral director will be present. It's a waste, except in the case of religious or traditional preferences, whereby the religion prefers the witnessing of the cremation by the family.

If you want to pay more, you can have a funeral service with the cremated remains just like a real funeral; but in this case instead of the gathered people gazing upon that nice mahogany casket, they get to see a box sitting on a pedestal. Again, this is an instance where no funeral director is required. Do your own, at your church, home, or favorite bar because it's really a memorial service unless you think that your deceased loved one's entire body is really in that little box; sorry, it's just some ground-up bone. The funeral home will push you to use their chapel because they want that extra eight hundred dollars. It might be convenient, but it's going to cost you.

The most expensive cremation option is where there is a funeral before the cremation. Yes, a full-sized funeral; now you have choices and decisions to make as above, just like a full-body funeral because it *is* a full-body funeral, except the body will stay with the funeral home to be cremated later. You can even add a graveside service after the cremation process (for more money because such a service would be a different scheduled event) to fully complete your funeral experience.

If you're going to have a preburn funeral service, you need a casket, but not just any casket, a cremation casket. And the funeral home is more than willing to sell you a nice box that will end up on the barbeque in a few days.

A cremation casket has very few metal parts and is designed specifically for cremation. After your funeral service, the deceased and casket go into the retort and are burned. The funeral home will sell you anything from a simple plywood box, nicely stained, to a very expensive cherrywood casket. Now the salesperson will tell you that a cherrywood casket will show the world how much you honor and cherish the deceased. It might also make a statement as to how much money you have and are willing to throw away. But it doesn't need to be that way. An alternative is the rental casket; that's right, you can rent a casket.

A rental casket will cost far less than a cremation casket. The rental casket is made of a wood, such as oak, with a removable interior plywood box; it's a casket within a casket. Remember, it's against the law to use a casket more than once per body. However, since a rental casket has a removable insert, the law against the reuse of a casket only applies to the insert. The foot of the rental casket opens down on a hinge. The plywood insert is removed with the body and then placed in the retort for cremation. A new insert is slid into the shell of the rental casket ready for the next customer. Upon inspection, you can't tell a rental casket from a regular wooden casket unless you know what you're looking for. The insert has the same "comfort" features and looks just like the interior of a regular casket.

It's important to understand that in most states, before cremation, the body has to be placed in a rigid container; hence, the cremation casket. But don't be fooled. Unless you're having a service before the cremation process, you don't need a cremation casket. What you need is a rigid, burnable container. The alternative is the "alternative container," a little play on words. The alternative container is simple: a seven-foot long cardboard box. You can supply your own container as long as it conforms to the crematory's standards. But don't aggravate yourself over that; get the alternative container supplied by the funeral home. The alternative container is usually bundled into the price of a "direct cremation" anyway. If not, the alternative container is not expensive, about forty-five dollars. I know it's expensive for a cardboard box; but, after all, you're dealing with the funeral industry.

We now have covered the essentials of prearranging funeral services, whether it involves a body or just a cremation and a box. Sure, you can prearrange such services as being compressed into a diamond, shot into low-orbital space (when the capsule reenters the earth's atmosphere your father will be cremated again). Plus, you can have some of your dad's ashes built into jewelry, snippets of hair placed into a locket, or dad's cremains placed in the base of a sundial. There are many options; but remember, it's what you want, not what someone can sell you, that counts. You want to create good memories on your terms. Simply put, you have two options—either Dad will be buried or cremated; everything else is just superfluous.

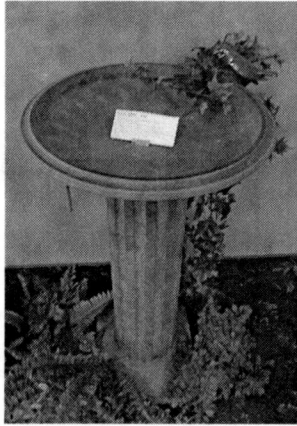

Chapter IV

Other Things to Know about Prearranging

"If I had known that, I wouldn't have done it"
—Famous Last Words

It's not about the funeral or cemetery. It's about the money, as well as about how you and your family feel regarding the final disposal of a loved one and what you want done if anything to honor that loved one. Therefore, you should keep some things in mind when considering prearrangements for yourself or a loved one. Always remember that to the funeral home, and especially the salesperson, this is a sales transaction, nothing more. They don't care if Uncle Joe was a convicted child predator, used car salesman, or Nobel Peace Prize winner. To them, it's a sale; and they measure how well they did their job by how much they were able to sell to you.

Another thing: some people think that for whatever reason, the county or state will pay for funeral arrangements, or at least a direct cremation. Not so. It is the responsibility of the next of kin to pay for funeral services, merchandise, and cemetery costs. Whoever is in control of the body at the time of death is monetarily responsible, and the state won't chip in. It's your kin, your money. So plan and save beforehand in order not to have your relatives blindsided with a two thousand dollar or greater bill. There are some exceptions to this rule, which I will go over later.

When prearranging a funeral and/or cemetery plot, try (and it might be hard to do) to leave the emotional baggage at the door. Pre-need salespeople will play on that emotional baggage, whether the arrangement is for you or for someone else.

The following is what you need:

1. Someone to pickup the deceased
2. Refrigeration and/or embalming, (embalming if required or you choose it)
3. A casket or urn if you need or choose to have one
4. Funeral or memorial service if you want either
5. Cremation if you choose it
6. A final resting place if you wish one
7. A death certificate

Everything else is fluff. And it's the fluff that the salesman wants you to buy. Remember, the salesperson has the items you need in hand. In other words, you will have to buy certain services from a funeral home in order to dispose of the body. It's up to you to decide how you're going to dispose of the body and how far you want to take the services and honoring part in order to satisfy *your* needs, not his. But if you leave the emotions at the door and remember the salesperson's motivation, you will spend less.

I can't say enough about shopping. Should you decide to prearrange funeral or cemetery needs, you have the time to shop, shop and shop. Should you not prearrange, you are under pressure to decide early about which funeral home you want to handle the arrangements because now you have an at-need situation. You can't let Uncle Joe just rot in his bed at home. Know this: each and every person will eventually need the services of a funeral home. Be prepared.

If you're under fifty, in good health, and you have no relatives over fifty, don't prearrange because statistically, you won't die for now. However, if you're under fifty and do things like jump over the Grand Canyon on a motorcycle or sky dive, you might want to reconsider. For the rest of us, looking into prearrangement is a very good idea since it gives you a plan. Don't end up making funeral arrangements at the last moment and having less planning time than it took to plan that cruise with the kids on the Disney liner in the Caribbean.

Here's a simple way of breaking down the way and type of planning one should do. For instance, you're over fifty, or you have relatives over fifty that you have some responsibility for, or someone in your family is in poor health, therefore:

1) You've got more money than God and you don't care how much you pay: so plan, but don't pay a prearrangement contract.

2) You only have enough money to keep hearth and home, but not a nickel to spare: so plan but don't pay a prearrangement contract.

3) You have some extra money, but not enough to pay for all the arrangements. Most importantly, you don't have the discipline to save your extra money for this life-ending event: so plan and pay the prearrangement contract over time, thereby freezing the price.

4) You have extra money, but not enough to pay for all the arrangements. However, you do have the discipline to put that extra money away over time to cover the eventual costs: so plan and don't pay a prearrangement contract; bank the money instead.

5) You have enough money socked away so that you can afford to pay for the whole enchilada, and it won't hurt you financially: so plan and pay it all, thereby freezing the price.

Let me explain.

Notice that I tell all of you, except those too young, to plan. You can plan, but you don't have to pay. All funeral homes will help you plan for your own or your parent's final send off without payment. They will advise you to put some money down on the plan because, if you don't, they really haven't made a sale, therefore a commission. But if forced to, and you *can* force them, they will plan a funeral or give you cemetery options as an unfunded plan. If they don't, you're in the absolutely wrong place.

Unfunded funeral/cemetery plans allow you to plan all the things you want without paying for those services and merchandise. It allows for your family to know what you or Aunt Mildred wants at the time of death, thus relieving family from all the decision making and potential mistakes. Should you do an unfunded funeral/cemetery plan, at the end of the planning session you should have a copy of the plan, and the funeral home will keep a copy for themselves. Let your next of kin know where that plan is in case you drop dead from eating that extra bowl of ice cream. The funeral home is motivated because you or your family will probably (not guaranteed) come back when the time comes. The beauty of an unfunded plan is that you are under no obligation to the funeral home. The downside to an unfunded plan is that the funeral home will call periodically to see if you want to start funding the plan and you haven't frozen the price since you've not put your hard earned money down on anything as of yet.

So you have lots of money and the cost of a funeral and burial will mean nothing to you or your family. As I said before, plan the funeral. Let your family know what your plans are, but keep your money. Your money will earn more and do more elsewhere rather than sitting in a funeral trust fund. On the other hand, if you haven't got enough to rub two sticks together and Dad is eighty and might not live to ninety, plan, but don't buy. Never pay for something you can't afford or that will hurt you month after month financially. Plan cheap, because when the time comes, the next of kin, usually the spouse or children, are responsible for payment. Perhaps you can warn others in the family as to what the plan is, and maybe they'll chip in. But do something. The time will come and you must be prepared.

Say you're in a position to make a plan and start to pay for the services you want. Then pay, but make the payments fit your financial picture. You'll need to put some money down and arrange to make monthly payments. If you're lucky, the person for whom you are paying this plan will live longer than it takes to pay off the plan. If the person dies before the plan is paid off, you'll have to come up with the balance immediately. However, say you're in the same position whereby you have extra money to pay for the funeral plan, but you have very good control and discipline over your finances. Then do an unfunded plan and set the monthly payment aside in your own bank. It will earn more interest than if set aside in a funeral trust, hopefully covering the subsequent price increases.

Finally, if you have enough money stashed away for the funeral services and merchandise you want and you just want to pay the thing off and take advantage of the guaranteed prices, then plan and pay. The money will go into a funeral trust fund and won't earn much interest, but that's not your problem. Should the person you're planning for live for ten or more years, you'll probably beat the system. Since the costs are frozen from the time you put your money down, the funeral home can't charge you more except for items that are marked non-guaranteed, such as the death certificate, memorial folders, and other miscellaneous items. The funeral home must deliver the services and merchandise you picked out or the equivalent should the item no longer be available.

Remember, if you're prearranging, you have time to shop. Call funeral homes and get pricing. Better yet, visit funeral homes and get a feel for their professionalism. You want to feel warm and cozy with the funeral home you choose. The last thing you want is to choose a cheap (or expensive) funeral home that will screw up your loved one's last hurrah. And believe me it happens all the time.

Okay, you're real clever; you think you can dodge all this planning by donating your body to "science." No, you have to plan for that and not just by telling your wife that anatomical donation is what you want. Should you plan for an anatomical donation, you need a funeral home. The funeral home will probably charge you the price that you would have paid for "forwarding remains to another funeral home" without the casket. Most anatomical donations are embalmed, not because the funeral home requires the embalming, but because the anatomical accepting authority will most likely require the embalming. But here's the real kicker: you might think it a fine idea to donate your body now; but when you die ten or twenty years from now, the accepting authority (usually a teaching hospital) may reject your body. They can reject you based on their needs (too many bodies), relative health of the deceased (communicable diseases), and/or condition of the body (such as morbid obesity or smashed into a pulp by a fallen bridge). So guess what? Your family is back to square one. Plan your donation; but also have a backup plan, just in case you're rejected.

But how about the disposition of indigents or the homeless? They don't need to plan, nor do they have the money to pay for their disposal at the time of their death. You're right—you got me on that, but the funeral home (in many states) that gets stuck with a homeless person's body is going to move heaven and earth to find the next of kin in order to pay for that disposition. If the funeral home can't locate a responsible party or should a next of kin refuse to pay for the disposition, the funeral home may be forced, by law in some states, to offer him or her up to the nearest medical school for anatomical donation. Should he or she be rejected or accepted, the county or state may pay the funeral home to have the deceased transported to the medical school or cremated depending on the decision. After which they're gonzo. When I sold my funeral home, I had ten homeless people all wrapped up in their cardboard boxes sitting in a locked cabinet. After one year, if no next of kin had claimed these cremated remains, they were to be scattered to the four winds.

Many funeral homes will not take indigent decedents because of the time, energy, and loss of money indigent disposal creates. Should a funeral home be paid by the county or state, its owners will be lucky to recover their costs but in all likelihood will lose money. My funeral home never turned down an indigent disposition simply because we felt it was our community duty.

Veterans

At this point, I would like to sincerely thank each and every veteran who has served our country; however, service to country doesn't mean veterans get a free funeral. Unless you're "Killed In Action" or in another service related accident, the government will not pay for your funeral services and merchandise. So, again you need to plan; however, should you so desire, you will receive a free cemetery plot, marker, grave liner, and grave opening and closing. You can be delivered to the cemetery for full body or cremated remains interment. Yet there are drawbacks to the free cemetery.

First, you have to be a veteran, honorably discharged with a DD214 form to prove so. All veterans know to keep their DD214 (discharge papers) in a safe place and to let others in their family know where the form is located. This form allows you to be buried in a national cemetery of your choosing. The downside to this is that the closest national cemetery may be hundreds of miles from your home. By the way, if you want to be buried at Arlington National Cemetery, you have to be a person of significant historical interest, to have reached a certain rank in the military, or to have gained certain honors while serving. So, for most of you, Arlington is out. For more information about Arlington burials and urn placements go to arlingtoncemetery.org.

Next, you don't get to pick out where in the cemetery you will be placed. Your grave placement will be in the area of the cemetery where they are currently digging graves. At the time of this writing, many World War II vets are passing away, and these national cemeteries are very busy, which leads us to scheduling. At the time of death, your funeral director will try to schedule a time with the cemetery that is good for both your family (if they choose to attend) and the cemetery. Should you schedule a graveside service at a national cemetery, you get fifteen minutes; and you better be on time because they will start without you if you're late. If you or your family chooses not to attend a graveside ceremony at a national cemetery, the funeral home will deliver the deceased to the cemetery to be buried at the leisure of the cemetery.

Another drawback to the national cemetery route is that if you want to be interred with a lot of family, forget it. National cemeteries only allow for the interment of the veteran, spouse, and any dependent children. Should you have a dependent child who predeceases you, that child could be buried in a national cemetery. Don't worry; they will make room for you and your spouse later in order to keep you all together. However, adult children of veterans are not allowed in national cemeteries, nor are divorced spouses.

So if you choose to go the national cemetery way, you don't have to plan for cemetery, gravesite, and merchandise; but you still have to plan how to get to the cemetery.

Funeral and Cemetery Trusts and Insurance

Now that you have decided on a cemetery and funeral arrangements, you need to pay for it unless you fit into one of the categories above that are better off postponing payment. Whether you decide to pay in full or monthly, is, of course, up to you. But you might want to know where the money is going since the funeral home is not delivering services or products until the death has occurred.

As in most things, it depends. The money for nondelivered items will go into a trust or insurance (which I will describe below). There are two categories of trust: revocable and nonrevocable, meaning the former can be canceled and the latter can't be canceled. The only reason to make the trust nonrevocable is that the beneficiary (the person the merchandise and services are provided for) is going on government assistance and you don't want the government to take away that asset. You can convert a revocable trust to a nonrevocable trust at anytime, but you can't undo a nonrevocable trust.

If you have purchased or started to pay for a gravesite, niche, or mausoleum crypt, this is cemetery merchandise that is considered delivered. In this case, the cemetery gets your money and keeps it. You can get your money back on everything else purchased because it hasn't been delivered. A small percentage of the grave, niche, or mausoleum purchase price is kept in trust if the cemetery is a perpetual cemetery whereby it is promised that the cemetery owners will maintain the cemetery (and therefore your plot) in perpetuity. The theory is that enough money will be in trust to maintain the cemetery when the cemetery closes (ceases to sell any more spaces). Most cemeteries are perpetual; however, there are some cemeteries that are not perpetual, and you must decide if you mind that your final resting place might lie in ruins twenty or hundred years from now. These cemetery trusts are controlled by the cemetery or its corporate headquarters (hence, occasional yet rare theft), and the state can audit such trusts at anytime.

Cemetery sales trusts are separate from funeral sales trusts. For all funeral sales, unless you decide to take your casket home and use it as a coffee table until needed, nothing can be delivered since no one has died yet. Therefore, almost all monies are placed in trust. The trust in this case exists to hold the money for your funeral services until time of death. The money will generate interest, which will theoretically off set the increase in costs to the funeral home over time. In other words, a casket that costs the funeral home three hundred dollars today will cost more a year from now. And, don't ever expect a funeral home to refund to your family any money that is generated by the trust which outmatches any increase in cost to them. They want to keep any extra, which will in all likelihood, be very small or nonexistent. However, should someone have prearranged thirty years prior to their demise, you might ask the funeral director how much is in the trust fund and then compare it to the funeral home's current cost. If there is more money in the trust fund than the current cost of the services that were contracted thirty years ago, ask for a refund of the difference. In all likelihood, you'll find that the trust fund grew at a slower pace than the costs the provider (funeral home) charges currently.

Additionally, at the beginning of each year that the trust is still in your name, as purchaser, hence owner, you will be responsible for any taxes incurred by the interest generated by your trust. Yep, each year you'll get a K-1 from the company that runs your trust in order to report the income to Uncle Sam. Don't be alarmed; the income is so low that it's unlikely to add to your yearly tax liability.

Should you go with one of the large national corporations, you can transfer the trust to any of their locations. However, should the prices be higher at the new location, they will want the difference. On the other hand, should the prices be lower, you most likely won't get a refund check for the difference voluntarily. Demand the difference anyway; you'll probably get it if you threaten to cancel the trust.

Remember, all monies held in trust by the funeral home or cemetery is your money. You, the purchaser, have complete control over the money and may cancel your arrangements at anytime. The only exception is irrevocable or nonrevocable trusts, delivered products such as the gravesite, or an urn on which you happen to take delivery. Should you decide to cancel, you should receive all your money back, plus interest, even if you've been making monthly payments. The funeral home/cemetery will make every effort to keep you from canceling, especially the salesperson who, if he is still working at the facility, sold you the products and services. They never want to lose the sale or especially the commission. They may go as far as telling you that you can't cancel, an outright lie. It might take ten to fifteen minutes to convince them you're serious about canceling. An important exception to canceling your trust or purchases is the gravesite. Once you put down your first nickel on that plot of land, it's yours. So, if you want to cancel, or worse, stop paying on the gravesite, the cemetery will just take it back and not refund any monies to you. It's like the repossession of a car when you stop making payments.

Should your funeral home, or for that matter the cemetery, be sold, all trusts will be transferred to the new owner. The new owner will contact you in order to inform you of the change in ownership. A change in ownership will not affect your trust; but there have been instances where the new owner has tried to bilk prearranged customers of the old owner. The new owner will either refuse to honor the contract or claim that he didn't know he had to honor the prearranged contract that came with the purchase of the funeral home or cemetery. That claim is ludicrous.

If, on the other hand, your funeral home goes belly-up, there are a couple of scenarios that can take place. First, the bankrupted funeral home or its receivers could sell the prearranged contracts to one or more funeral homes for a very much reduced face value of the contracts (pennies on the dollar). The purchasing funeral home will then notify you of the change and honor the contract. Second, should there be no buyer for the contracts (not a likely scenario), the trust will be refunded back to the purchaser along with any accumulated interest. Third, should you feel nervous about the new owner of the contract, you may cancel your prearranged contract.

At many funeral homes, especially the corporate held funeral homes, you will find that most, if not all, the pre-need salespeople hold a life insurance license. The reason? Increase in commissioned sales. Yup, there is burial insurance to be had and the pre-need salesperson wants to sell you that policy. The good news is that the cost of your funeral and merchandise will be the same as if you bought with cash or made payments into a trust. Additionally, most of these burial insurance policies are transferable. In other words, a policy bought through one funeral home will be, in all likelihood, accepted by most other funeral homes. Why? It's a guaranteed payoff for the funeral home.

The pre-need salesperson loves to do burial insurance because the insurance company will usually pay a higher commission than the funeral home itself. Some of the big funeral corporations sell their own burial/life insurance, and there are several insurance companies that are independent of the funeral industry which sell burial insurance. When I owned my own funeral home, an insurance company begged us to sell their funeral and burial insurance policies. The incentive was very good because they would advertise and market our funeral home. On top of that, the "salesperson" could augment his or her income from the sales of such policies. As tempting as the offer was, we chose not to sell burial/life insurance policies since no one on staff was considered a salesperson much less a commissioned salesperson. Commissioned sales were considered a conflict of interest, and therefore no insurance policy was ever sold by my funeral home.

Should you be one of those who choose to plan for their funerals but do not pay for the plan, you can use any life insurance policy to pay for the funeral at the time of need. For instance, say that you've planned cemetery and funeral services for your father but decided that now was not the time to pay for such services. However, your father has a large life insurance policy. At the time of his demise, you can assign the cost of the cemetery, funeral, and merchandise to the funeral home from the life insurance policy. Provided the beneficiary or beneficiaries make such assignment and the policy is assignable, there is no funeral home that I know of that would turn such an assignment down. In fact, many funeral homes will wait for the policy to pay out to the family without assignment, depending on how much the mortuary trusts the family. At the same time, the funeral home will want to confirm such a policy exists.

Chapter V

What Goes on behind the Prearrangement Sales Office Door

It's Dog Eat Dog.

My experience on the sales side of the cemetery and funeral business was a shock and horrification of my good common sense. Now, remember, I can only relate what I experienced; however, from talking with others in the industry, my experiences are common throughout the business. With the exception of some, the problems of the sales departments and the funeral business as a whole are generated by the people and by the manner of their compensation. As I stated at the beginning, I have never been associated with a group of people who guarded their "professionalism" so diligently while being the epitome of nonprofessional.

Straight commission salespeople are not greedy and do not want to cause the customer harm, but they are desperate. Because of the way they're paid, they become greedy and will harm their customers. The more they sell, the more they get paid. They have to up-sell, hammer the customer to buy more than the customer requires or wants because the salespeople never know where their next sale will come from or when it will come. Unfortunately, the businesses that choose to use straight commission salespeople have created this atmosphere by the very nature in which the business compensates the salesperson. The commission pay structure attracts a work force which in many cases is slovenly, poorly educated, sometimes self-destructive, and desperate. Most people don't and won't work for commission only unless they're very good at it or desperate, at least not at this pay level. Thus, this form of pay lends itself to bringing in people that are not skilled and are more or less unemployable. Think about it: in many big-box stores you find an assortment of young people selling clothes, electronics, sporting gear, or other items. These people are for the most part nonskilled and not college educated. Management is asking you to believe some twenty year old with a cheap tie in the electronics department is the expert you're going to rely upon to give you informed information on your three thousand dollar plasma television. Chances are that in a year, that kid will be long gone, not because he or she didn't work hard or is not intelligent, but because he or she couldn't make a living selling on mostly or strictly commission. Additionally, ask yourself how excited can one get given the opportunity to work at a funeral home or cemetery. Many people wouldn't even consider the idea. How excited would you be to work five days a week calling one hundred of your friends and neighbors and asking them if they wanted to buy a cemetery plot? Therefore, for the most part, you'll find the dregs.

The funeral industry likes this arrangement. There is little money plowed into their salespeople by way of training. They don't sell, they don't get paid. If a salesperson doesn't sell enough, he gets canned. There's always someone to take his place. Very few benefits are available to the salesperson since he or she is considered an independent contractor or, at best, a part-time employee. Some funeral home/cemetery combo units will hire up to a hundred salespeople and telemarketers. The thinking is that if you throw enough spaghetti at the wall, something will stick. It's a horrible situation. There are not enough dollars generated by sales for such a work force. Therefore, a revolving door is created. Very few are making a living, so most will leave after a relatively short period.

The upshot: creation of an atmosphere where cheating, dishonesty, fights--both physical and verbal, theft, desperation, and fraud are the order of the day; and the managers of such workplaces won't and can't change the situation. It's important for you as the consumer to know about this atmosphere, since such knowledge will enable you to deal with your salesperson more effectively. Again, it's not about the funeral, but about your money and the rather large purchase you're contemplating. Such knowledge will give you power.

When you walk into a funeral home or cemetery sales office, you will be greeted in a friendly way. An atmosphere of kindness and cooperation drips from the place. However, right when you open your mouth, you'll be asked if you are working with someone already. That question is to find out if you are an open lead. There are some rules to being a commission only salesperson; one is thou shall not steal another's customer. Yet, if one can steal another's customer, one will. At the funeral home, there will be one or two salespeople on duty. In other words, one salesperson gets all the pre-need phone inquiries and walk-ins during the day, namely, the pre-need salesperson. This is his best time to generate new leads. There may or may not be another salesperson on duty whose job is to sell merchandise to families that are coming in for at-need reasons. There will be other salespeople at the funeral home who are not on duty, but banging the phones for new leads, meeting with previously generated leads, or just hanging out to avoid the wife and kids. What the on-duty pre-need salesperson has to worry about are these off-duty salespeople because they can snag a potential walk-in customer just by being at the door and later claiming that the customer was a self-generated lead.

Even better is the salesperson who (this has been done) bribes the receptionist, who in turn directs all the phone inquiries to his extension. This can happen with the knowledge of the sales manager who receives a commission override on all sales no matter who generated the sale. He doesn't care that the on-duty salesperson won't be generating any leads and therefore not feeding his or her family. It doesn't hurt that the guy bribing the receptionist is also the most aggressive salesperson in the office, therefore posting the largest sales numbers. Large sales numbers are good for business and good for the sales manager who must make sales goals. Another variation of bribing the receptionist is to give a kickback on every sales lead generated by a telemarketer. This way the salesperson creates his own private telemarketing department.

Usually there is a rule protecting your leads. For instance, should a salesperson develop a lead and that customer show up without an appointment while the lead developing salesperson is absent, another salesperson is to help the customer and not lay claim to a commission. Unfortunately, that rule doesn't always hold up because it's easy for the covering salesperson to make the sale and not tell the salesperson that developed the lead in the first place. Hence, an atmosphere of deception, thievery, and lies is generated. This is bad for you, the consumer, because if the salespeople can't be honest with each other, they're not going to be honest with you. Salespeople will protect their files and leads since other salespeople will look through them or even steal them.

That happened to me on several occasions, but the one that finally got me to act had to do with a sale I had been working on for months. This was a big sale consisting of a couple of crypts and funeral services. My clients finally decided to do the deal and just walked in, without an appointment, on a Sunday when I wasn't at the office. The clients asked for me and were informed I wasn't there, but the thief on duty told them not to worry, "we all work together." He wrote up my deal and pocketed the commission. I found out several days later what happened when I called the client and asked if they had decided to purchase the crypts. When I confronted the thief, I told him that if he ever talked to me, much less stole one of my clients, I would consider it an assault and destroy him. The thief not only apologized, but credited his future sales and commissions to make up my loss, equaling the amount he stole from me. (Remember, I, too, have to reach monthly sales goals.) Will I trust him again? Never, and you shouldn't either.

Salespeople are hammered by management everyday to sell more. There are never enough sales. The sales manager is pressured by upper management to ever increasing monthly sales. That's why sales managers will hire more salespeople than the unit can possibly need in order to get more people on the phone soliciting sales. Hence, more people not making a living. Hence, more people not making their sales goals. Hence, more desperate salespeople. Hence, more sales by deception. The sales manager doesn't care; he only wants the sales goal to be reached every month. It's his bread and butter. The sales manager doesn't mind that his most successful salesperson is a cocaine addict or an alcoholic, because he's the most successful salesperson. Upper management doesn't care that the unit posted its highest sales figures ever; for the next month, they expect more; hence, more pressure on everyone. You as a salesperson had better post your sales goals consistently or you're out; your replacement will be in tomorrow. Hence, a revolving door of poorly trained, poorly educated, and desperate people. Morale is never high. You as the consumer will pay for this unless you are prepared and understand the atmosphere.

Training is nonexistent. Salespeople learn on the job. Although, selling of funerals, merchandise, and cemetery plots is not rocket science, you do need to know how things work and what is doable. But training, which in turn would make the salesperson much more professional, takes time, energy, and money. Since the sales manager doesn't know from one day to the next if his new hire will come back, there's little need to train. What training is given involves how to sell more and overcome objections to the sale. Scripted sales guides are handed out in order for a salesperson to overcome the "no" that most customers give when called out of the blue. But ethics are not part of the deal. The funeral home and the sales manager don't encourage fraud or deceitful tactics; they just don't want to know about it.

In my experience, some of the people were so desperate that they stole from the company. All money, checks, and credit card receipts were dropped into a lockbox and retrieved the next day. One day, one of our "better" salesmen concluded a prearranged package that cost over six thousand dollars. The customers paid in cash. Well, this salesman wasn't satisfied with the commission he would earn, which was over six hundred dollars. He wanted it all. He devised a scheme whereby he would drop the money at the end of the day, but he would leave part of the envelope which contained the cash just visible and able to be reached by a coat hanger. Another salesman would retrieve the envelope and both would split the cash. This "Thomas Crown Affair" was executed flawlessly. But I instantly knew who did the dirty deed by a) knowing the character and personality of my fellow coworkers, b) knowing the motivation of both (one was desperate because he hadn't closed a sale in three weeks, the other needed the money for reasons I won't divulge here), and c) one quit the day that the general manager announced lie-detector tests for all. Naturally, no one could prove anything, and the company was too frightened of its own shadow to fire the perpetrators and never did the lie detector test. But everyone knew who did it. The point is this: how can you trust a salesman who would steal from his own employer? He's going to steal from you.

Yet, there are some in sales who won't stoop to underhanded sales tricks and deceptions. There are people in the industry who work hard, are honest, and truly want to help you; and they tend to be long-term employees. But you don't know who the honest and straightforward ones are as opposed to the untrained desperate salespeople. Therefore, it's best to be aware of what goes on behind the sales office door in order to more effectively deal with your salesperson and protect your wallet. You might want to ask the salesperson how long he or she has worked with the company. Also, enquire if the person has bounced around from funeral home to funeral home, if so, there maybe a reason. Be aware, be educated, and ask questions. Don't be lured into purchases for the sake of memorializing. All honoring and memorializing suggestions should come from you, not the salesperson. Remember, to the salesperson, it's not about the funeral. Decide pretty much what you want before you meet with a salesperson. Shop, shop, shop! Be comfortable with the salesperson before you buy. If you don't like the salesperson you get, ask for another or go somewhere else. And if you read and retain the information in this book, you'll probably know more about the funeral business than the average pre-need salesperson. It's your money, your funeral, and you have the right to decide.

After two years as a pre-need salesperson, my sales manager got promoted to corporate. Before he made his announcement that he was leaving our unit, he asked to see me in private. He told me that he was leaving and that another salesman was going to be made sales manager. He asked if I would become assistant sales manager. This request came as a shock since I was barely performing at expectations and had been planning to give my two weeks notice. I had had enough, and I certainly didn't need the money. I told the sales manager that I would give him an answer in two weeks.

After two weeks of agonizing reflection, I took the job as assistant sales manager without an increase in compensation; in other words, I was still just a commission salesperson. Instead of quitting, I had hoped to make a difference. I had one qualification I insisted on before taking on the job: all hiring and firing, plus any major sales policy decision had to have my input since in my opinion the new sales manager was way over his head and dishonest to boot. The outgoing and new sales managers agreed, for all the good it did me.

Three days after I took the new position, I walked into the telemarketer's office, which was a trailer separate from the main building, and was told that I was in charge of the telemarketing department. I was surprised since the sales manager had not told me, but maybe I could make a difference there. The telemarketing group was very small and very demoralized. They were told almost daily that they would lose their jobs if they couldn't generate more leads for the sales department.

I had them run some numbers for me and found that out of the hundreds of calls made daily, only 0.7 percent generated any kind of positive response. That was wasting time and I changed things. There would be no more cold calls and from now on only calls to people we had a reason to call, in other words, people who had done business with us before. The result? The telemarketing group went from near zero sales per month to thirty-two thousand dollars the first four weeks after I took over. This actually did not please my new sales manager because I didn't have the telemarketers make hundreds of calls a day, and I think it must have intimidated him.

Then one day I was walking by an arrangement room where I notice the sales manager interviewing a potential salesperson. Our agreement was that I would be a part of every hiring decision, but here he was excluding me. I walked in on the interview and participated despite his obvious irritation. After interviewing the obviously desperate potential employee, I objected, in the strongest terms, to hiring this person. Two days into the job, this new hire was threatening a sexual harassment suit against the company and sales manager.

It was then I decided that I couldn't make a difference, and it was time to leave. And leave I did; the last month I was there, I purposely sold nothing. I took myself off the duty list, made no appointments, and avoided my clients. I think I went into the office a total of seven days for the whole month. The result—our new sales manager managed to miss the monthly sales goal for the first time in fourteen months. He didn't last nine months; but I didn't care. I was gone.

Here again, I was footloose and fancy free. As an employee with the company, I had thought many times: what if there was a funeral home offering superior service without exploiting those in need, making it more about the funeral. It was my feeling that marketing the funeral home properly without up-setting many people in turn would yield fair and growing profits. So I founded my own funeral home, became a funeral director, and jumped into the world of at-need.

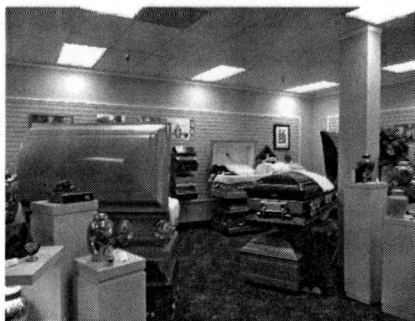

Chapter VI

At Need

"Good-bye cruel world--it's over; walk on by."

- Pink Floyd

Choosing a Funeral Home, Who Is Responsible, and the Last Ride

So Aunt Mildred's at the hospital; they've done all that they can. She decides, "I can do better," and dies, croaks, buys the farm, checks out, expires, passes away, passes on, whatever—she's dead. Who do you call? Not ghost busters; they can't help. But the hospital has to call someone. Hopefully you and/or your aunt decided on whom before she went to play bingo with God.

As I said before, shop, shop, and shop some more. Most deaths are not a surprise, but on occasion, we are caught unaware. An auto accident, sudden heart attack, drug overdose, industrial accident, whatever it may be; we might be dealing with a death that totally blindsides us. And here's the problem, you and your family will be a total emotional wreck. The funeral home knows this and will act accordingly. Unfortunately, you will have to make decisions under this emotional stress; and in all likelihood, it will cost you.

Now, in the event of a death, whether it's at home, an accident, at the hospital, at a nursing home, out in the great outdoors, or under the care of hospice, someone will notify the medical examiner within the county in which the death occurred. It is up to the medical examiner to decide if he or she wants to release the body or keep the deceased for examination. In most cases the medical examiner's office will release the body immediately. Even in the event of a sudden death, the medical examiner may issue a release should the cause of death be obvious.

Should the medical examiner keep your loved one for a day or two, you will have time to shop around for a funeral home that you feel comfortable handling the arrangements. However, once the medical examiner has finished the autopsy or other tests, the medical examiner's office wants your loved one out.

When shopping for a funeral home and/or cemetery, first use the phone. You can call a funeral home twenty-four hours a day and ask questions. After hours, you'll get an answering service. The answering service will screen your call and then put you through to a representative of the funeral home, in most cases a funeral director. However, if the person representing the funeral home can't or won't answer your questions, even at three in the morning, find another funeral home. But, you may ask, what am I looking for in a funeral home, especially in the middle of the night? What you want, or at least what I would want, is someone who is kind, gentle, patient, and who treats your situation as if it is the most important thing in the world—because to you it is the most important thing in the world. What you don't want is someone on the other end of the phone who comes across as disinterested, put-upon, or gruff and assumes he has the business just by answering the phone.

The funeral director should immediately ask how he or she can help you. This allows you to explain your situation and circumstances as you want. As you get deeper into the conversation, the funeral director may start asking for more details, such as where the decedent is and if the medical examiner has been notified. But don't let him assume he has your business before you're ready to give him the case. Make him earn your business by earning your trust. If you ever get a "funny feeling" or you're not clicking, say thank you and good-bye.

No funeral home should ever assume it has the case. If its representatives assume too much, they can be burned. For instance, a gentleman died at a nursing home he had lived at for several months. His death occurred at two o'clock in the morning, and the nursing home could not locate the family; therefore, the nursing home assumed the funeral home down the street would do handsomely. The funeral home sent out two first call personnel. Unfortunately, the decedent was rather large, so the funeral home had to call outside help in order to complete the removal.

The nursing home finally located the family, who in turn went to the funeral home where this particular gentleman was taken. This family was smart; as they got into the final arrangement (cremation), they balked at the price. The family suspended the arrangement, made three phone calls, and chose my funeral home. We warned the family that the first funeral home would try to charge them for at least a removal fee; however, we also pointed out that since the family did not authorize the funeral home to make the removal, they really shouldn't have to pay for the removal. And that's what they told the funeral home, and the funeral home had to relent; the family wasn't charged for the removal. The funeral home was burned by the nursing home because the funeral home made the removal in good faith. Still the family did not and should not have paid.

You are not going to go over the detailed costs of a full-blown funeral at three in the morning. In order to get a handle on how competitive the funeral home is to others in the area, ask how much they charge for a direct cremation. This will give you an idea about who is overpriced, and yes, who might be too low. Be leery of super-low-cost funeral arrangements. Either it's a one man show, or they are leaving something out of the pricing. So, when asking for the price of a direct cremation, make sure you ask what the "direct cremation" includes. It should include removal of the deceased, all the paperwork, refrigeration, cremation process, and a temporary urn (cardboard or plastic box). The only additional cost to you should be death certificates, and in some places they will throw in the first death certificate as part of the price. Even if you're planning a funeral with burial to follow, comparison of direct cremation prices will give you an idea about who's charging too much.

Who has a right to make final arrangements for a decedent? When a person dies, unlike all other assets, the body is not part of the dead person's estate. Some of this is obvious; however, you should be aware of your rights and the rights of others. The right of possession and disposal of a body first goes to the legal current spouse. I have run into several instances where the decedent has been divorced or widowed and has lived with someone for several years but is not legally married. All of a sudden the children or other relatives show up for their inheritance and possession of the body. The person who lived with the deceased—nurturing, sharing, caring for all those years—is out; because he or she has no legal or blood bond with the deceased.

Should there not be a spouse, children of the deceased over the age eighteen are next in charge. Naturally, if there is more than one child, there can be a problem, especially for the funeral director handling the case. It doesn't happen often, but a fight over a body can get very ugly and in my opinion is not worth it. Children fighting over a decedent should take into consideration what the decedent wanted, if known. Attorneys can be very expensive, and in twenty years, no one will care if Mom was buried in California or Ohio.

Next in line, the parents of the deceased. Yup, parents still have some rights, and if the deceased has no spouse or children over the age eighteen it's the parents' right and duty. Should no parents survive the decedent, it's up to the siblings. Again, there can be battles, but it's not worth the trouble. The funeral director will attempt if need be to build a consensus. After the brothers and sisters are eliminated, any other relatives, hopefully by blood, get their whack at the body.

After blood relative ties are exhausted, a personal representative of the decedent is given the right to make decisions. This is someone who has known the decedent and has acted on behalf of the decedent. Should the decedent have signed a statement authorizing the personal representative to take control over the decedent's body, that representative may, in fact, supersede the rights of all others on the above list. However, I've never known a personal representative to try to supersede the rights of a legal spouse. If a personal representative should try to abrogate the rights of a spouse, as a funeral director, I would be on the phone to my attorney before proceeding.

If there is no relative or personal representative, the state or county may claim the body for anatomical purposes. In these events the funeral director must offer the body to the anatomical director of the state. This happens more in cases of the homeless where no one can be found to claim the body. This may occur when family is found, but will deny responsibility and forgo their rights to the body. Finally, after all the above is exhausted, should there be an interested party, that person may lay claim to the body and assume responsibility for its disposition.

Every once in awhile, you will hear of some fantastic fight over the body of a dead person. Anna Nicole Smith comes to mind. In my mind, Ms. Smith's body should have been disposed of according to the wishes of her mother. However, it appears the court presumed that Ms. Smith's wishes were to be buried next to her son in Bermuda. The court allowed that the deceased's presumed wishes superseded all other claims. As a funeral director, I would be happy to allow the attorneys to fight it out. Funeral directors do not want to be caught in the middle of family fights. They just want to be paid.

In any case, once it is determined who has rights to Aunt Mildred's body and which mortuary is going to be used, it's time to make that first call. Aunt Mildred's not going anywhere for a while if she or her family have decided to donate organs for transplant. But, sooner than later, the hospital will call the funeral home your Aunt Mildred or you picked out to arrange for her final disposition. Most of the time, when the hospital calls the funeral home, she'll already be in the hospital's cooler. Occasionally, she could be in the room where she passed away should the hospital not have a cooler. Sometimes families will ask that the deceased not be taken to the cooler, although that request is rarely made or granted. Most states allow only so much time for an unembalmed body to be left at room temperature. The hospital staff will tag and bag. The body bag used is not the one you see on television, but usually a white, lightweight, zippered plastic bag onto which they will tie a nametag. Aunt Mildred is placed on a gurney, wheeled to the service elevator, and taken to the cooler. The cooler is in a locked room. Sometimes, if the hospital has an autopsy room, the cooler will be located there. Upon arrival, she will be either left on the gurney (yes, coolers can be that big) or placed on a rack which has several levels of trays.

Once the funeral home is called by the hospital (the first call), the funeral home will send one or two people for the removal in an unmarked or very discreetly marked van. It will not send a hearse or coach since that vehicle is used in funerals and is expensive to run. Upon arrival, the first call people will check-in with the administration (usually bed control), then most likely drive to a loading dock from which they will access the cooler.

When the first call people reach the cooler, they will glove up unless they're stupid. Let's face it; no matter how nice and clean you and your family are, the first call people don't know the deceased from Adam. They don't know the cause of death. On top of that, there might be blood or other bodily fluids, so glove up they will. The first call people will then look at the tag on the bag, zip open the bag, and look at the hospital wristband to confirm the identity of the deceased. It would be a bad thing to get a body all the way to the funeral home just to find out you got the wrong person.

Next, the mortuary's cot is prepared to accept the body. The cot has a body bag on it that is opened and then draped over the sides of the cot. The bag is thick walled and has a zipper running the length of the bag. The exterior looks like a nice cloth material. It doesn't look like a body bag such as you see on television. Then, another white, lightweight plastic bag is draped over the cot and its outer bag. This is to keep the expensive outer cot bag from getting dirty or contaminated. Then the cot is brought up as close to the deceased as possible, and the body is lifted to the cot.

Now, let me tell you, I have never seen or heard firsthand of any disrespect for the deceased by any first call people or for that matter, any funeral home personnel. I have actually seen and heard of bodies that were accidentally bumped, or dropped—not out of disrespect or disregard, but by accident. After all, a dropped body just constitutes more work. No one wants to play with a body. However, there may be some comment such as the weight of a body or the manner of the death. After all, if you had to lift a three-hundred-pound dead body, you'd probably comment on the size of such a body (five hundred pounds is my record). Occasionally, you may hear of a funeral home or director caught up in a body parts selling scandal. But these instances are not due to disrespect: these people are in it for money and the selling of body parts without authorization from the family is illegal. A fascinating take on an illegal operation involving body part sales and corpse abuse is the book *Chop Shop* by K. Braidhill. Selling body parts, in my opinion, happens, though rarely, and it will make headlines if it should happen; corpse abuse I wouldn't worry too much about.

After the deceased is placed on the cot, the light liner bag is folded over the body, and the outer cot bag is folded over the body and zipped closed. Finally, the deceased is rolled to the waiting van, placed inside, the doors are closed and *locked*, any paperwork is signed, and any keys returned to bed control. And off Aunt Mildred goes to her favorite funeral home. Maybe. Some smaller funeral homes don't have a holding facility with a cooler. In that case the funeral home will share a holding facility with other funeral homes. The upside is that it holds (no pun intended) down a little of the overhead and up-front capital costs to the funeral home; thus, in theory at least, holding down the cost to you. The downside I will go into a little later; suffice to say, it can be an inconvenience.

Once she arrived at the funeral home's cooler, the outer bag is unzipped and folded down over the cot. The body is again tagged with the funeral home's own identity bracelet or tag, and the inner plastic bag is folded over the body and taped closed, whereupon a magic marker is used to write the last name of the decedent on the bag. In the case of a shared cooler, the name of the decedent and the name of the funeral home are written on the plastic bag. The cot is then wheeled next to a shelf or tray in the cooler, and the body is slid onto the shelf or tray from the cot.

At my funeral home, before we taped shut the inner bag, we took a thumbprint of the deceased, in case the family wished a "thumbie" to be made. That's right—the funeral industry has come up with a way to make a pendant with your loved one's actual thumb print. Our funeral home never pushed this item; but we did let families know that if they so chose, the "thumbie" could be made at any time in the future. We sold many "thumbies." Another reason for the print was to cover ourselves, just in case we were ever accused of snatching the wrong body. That never happened.

But say Aunt Mildred dies at home which includes nursing homes: what then? First, the family has to notify the authorities that there has been a death. If Aunt Mildred has been in the care of a physician, resident of a nursing home yet at home not in a hospital, or under hospice care at home or nursing home, the medical examiner will most likely release the body to the funeral home. However, if the death is sudden, accidental, or under suspicious circumstances, the medical examiner may want to autopsy. Nevertheless, the funeral home can't remove the body until it is released. Should you be the lucky person to notify the authorities, call the police, they in turn will notify the medical examiner. If Aunt Mildred is under hospice care, notify hospice and they will contact the medical examiner.

When the first call team comes to a private home, they will make contact with the family in the house. Then they will, if they are smart, examine the room, hallways, and any obstacles, such as stairs, of the decedent's home. Next, they will bring in the cot to the decedent's room. At this point, if they are considerate, they will ask the family if they are ready for the removal and if they want to watch; some do, some don't. Since no one has placed Aunt Mildred in a convenient plastic bag, the removal team will wrap her into a bed sheet that they brought with them. This is done by covering her with the sheet, rolling her onto one side while tucking part of the sheet under her back, rolling her on her other side and bringing the sheet out from under her and folding that portion of the sheet over her. Thus, a simple mummy wrap is completed. The same holds true for removal out of a nursing or assisted living home. Should the family be at the facility, the removal team will make contact with them. Sometimes family is present, sometimes not. The removal team won't expect family to remain at such a facility at three in the morning after a death, but sometimes they will stay until the removal is complete.

Some families want to complete the arrangements right there and then. Most funeral homes will not do this mainly because the removal teams a) don't have the proper paperwork with them, b) there is no director with the removal team, and c) the funeral home wants you in their facility in order to sell more services and products. My funeral home, however, always carried the paperwork with us to all removals for this eventuality. We believed the wishes of the family superseded our desire to remove the decedent. On the other hand, I personally felt that making and paying for final arrangements while the body was cooling in the front room was bad form. After all, there is a time and a place for everything.

Now if you think that in the middle of the night Joe Smith's Funeral and Burial Service is sending two people over to your house, that might not happen. Oh, someone will show up, but they may not work directly for Joe Smith's; they'll be with a first call company or work for the corporation that owns Joe Smith's and other funeral homes. The first call company eliminates the use of the funeral home's own employees for the mundane job of retrieving bodies. It's cheaper to send out lower paid people to do this job than to send your own. The first call people will make contact with the family and represent by inference that they work for the funeral home you have chosen. The first call company has the business cards of all the funeral homes they make first calls for, and cannot and will not make any arrangements on scene. Their only job is to remove the decedent and deliver the body to the funeral home that has called them to make the removal. The use of a first call service by your funeral home shouldn't make a difference to you. The only downside to you is that they won't be able to answer many of your questions since they have no knowledge of your situation and do not have the authorization to answer specific questions. What they will tell you is that the funeral home will be contacting you shortly to make an appointment to go over the final arrangements.

At my funeral home, we rarely used a first call service. We felt that it was important to give each family as much undivided attention as possible. However, once in awhile we would use a first call service if we were so busy that we couldn't respond in a reasonable amount of time. In addition, we would call them should we need extra help in the removal, such as the removal of a very large person.

Our policy was to be at the hospital, private home, or nursing facility within an hour after receiving the "first call." When a family has been up all night or holding a death vigil all day, they are tired. It is important that families feel the funeral home is concerned and responsive to their needs. But even more important are time and temperature. The moment someone dies, things begin to happen; and they're not good. I won't go into the physiology and biology of what is taking place both inside and outside the body; but suffice it to say, things are breaking down. The warmer the house, the faster bad things happen. Sick people tend to have unpleasant odors about them while alive. When they die, it gets worse; and as time goes on, it gets a lot worse.

Therefore, a good response time is a sign of an attentive funeral home.

For example, we picked up a man who had died around twelve thirty in the morning. The problem was we didn't arrive at the home until about eight thirty that morning. The fellow's wife had decided to spend one more night with her husband, and their two dogs in the same bed. She didn't call hospice until seven forty-five the next morning, who in turn called us. This was in the wintertime and the house was well heated. By the time we arrived, things were, needless to say, getting very ripe.

So, what happens next? Now that we know where Aunt Mildred is cooling her heels, someone is going to meet with the mortician (funeral director). The person responsible for the remains of Aunt Mildred will have to make final arrangements and/or go over the prearranged contract with the funeral director in order to dispose of Aunt Mildred's body

Chapter VII

The Arrangement

An Exercise in Hammering the Customer Revisited

After the first call team has done their little bit, you'll get a call from the funeral home, most likely from the funeral director who will be making the final arrangements with you. He or she will ask when it would be convenient for you to come in to make the final arrangements. All funeral homes want you to come to them. It makes selling and explaining the funeral plan much easier for the funeral director. Additionally, should the funeral home be located in a cemetery or memorial park, you will more than likely get an earful about why you should bury a casket or urn in their park. It's much easier to sell that nice casket, urn, or even a gravesite when those items are on display than from a book of pictures. At my funeral home, we always offered to visit the family if they so chose. This helps put the family at ease by being in their own familiar territory, but it costs money to send a funeral director to a private home; thus, it's not often offered. However, if you insist, they will come because they can't afford to lose you as a client.

When setting the appointment, make sure that it is at a time when you are well rested. If you've been up all night with the now departed, don't go in at nine o'clock in the morning exhausted from your ordeal.

Should you be emotionally distraught over the death, bring someone who is more removed from the death than you are. That person may not be making the final decisions, but will be more likely to spot emotional selling and may guide you away from spending your money on foolish items. Remember, except for some required charges, which should be explained by the funeral director, your planning of a funeral/memorial should be as you want it to be. In other words, you make the decisions as to how you want to memorialize and honor the deceased, not what the funeral director thinks you should do in this regard.

Before you go to the arrangement conference, make sure you have the following information and items:

1. Full name and address of the decedent. You would be surprised to know how many people don't know either the middle name of the decedent or their legal first name.
2. How long the decedent lived at his or her last address.
3. The decedent's usual occupation. "Retired" doesn't work; the county wants to know what the deceased did for a living over most of his or her life.
4. The decedent's highest level of education.
5. Social Security number—an absolute must unless the deceased is not a resident of the good old US of A.
6. Date and place of birth.
7. Military discharge papers—very important for veterans, especially if being interned within a national cemetery.
8. Father's name and birthplace—not yours, those of the deceased.
9. Mother's name and birthplace.
10. Insurance policies if used to pay for the arrangements.
11. Prearrangement and cemetery papers if any.

12. All necessary telephone numbers of those who must be contacted, such as church, pastor, lawyers, insurance companies, etc.
13. Clothes for the deceased to be buried in if not cremated.

Don't panic if you don't have some of the above-named items. Most of the information will be needed by the director when he fills out the death certificate. Sometimes items on the death certificate are blank because nobody knows, for instance, the decedent's mother's maiden name. But you should want to be as complete as possible. After all, it is an important document.

Upon arrival at the funeral home, you'll be ushered into an arrangement room. There you will find a table, chairs, perhaps a computer, and walls lined with merchandise. You'll be greeted by the funeral director who will say that he's sorry for your loss and offer you some refreshment, such as coffee or water. Don't count on any food, so be fed and content; the arrangement could last up to two hours or more. After some small talk and if you have not made any prearrangements, the question of the day will be asked, "Are you looking for burial or cremation?"

First we'll address the cremation arrangement. You've done some shopping around and believe the funeral home you've chosen is a reasonably priced funeral home. Let's say you've chosen a funeral home with an attached cemetery. Now you get to meet the tag team I mentioned early in the book. The funeral director will start you off by arranging for the services of the cremation, memorial, and any aspect that doesn't deal with the cemetery. What he wants to do is up-sell those services, try to divert you from something simple to a lavish send-off for the dear departed. After the funeral director is finished raking you over the coals, a "cemeterian," who is just a pre-need salesperson, will want to induce you to buy a space, urn, and other accoutrements in the cemetery.

So, here's how it will go: you just want to have a simple direct cremation and take the box home to put up on the fireplace mantle. But the funeral director will show you several optional packages which will include extra death certificates, maybe a flower allowance, memorial folders, and the like. Or, you could go big and really honor your loved one by choosing a more expensive package, which might include a full-blown funeral before cremation, flowers, minister, memorial cards, embalming. Most funeral homes have variations on the above themes. However, remember, all funeral homes have two packages which must be included in the general price list, immediate burial, and direct cremation. These two packages are the funeral home's lowest-priced services to get your loved one from the place of death to the crematory or hole in the ground. All the rest is just fluff.

On the other hand, if you see a package that has most, if not all, of the items you desire for a proper send-off, by all means, get the package. Item for item a package deal will be a better buy than the price for all the individual items added up from the general price list. However, if you are contemplating a package deal that has items you desire with items you don't want, and compare the general price list's individual price of the items you want against the package deal that has the wanted items and the unwanted items. You do the math.

If I were to have a cremation, I would just opt for a direct cremation with perhaps a decent urn. After the cremation process, I would hold a memorial service on my own at a time and place of my choosing. I would probably have the funeral home make some memorial folders, which will cost extra, but I don't want the hassle of trying to make them myself or of finding them on the Internet and having them come out not quite right. Remember, the one advantage of having a funeral home personnel do things and acquire merchandise for you is that they are accountable.

But should you decide that your family, friends, and the deceased desire to have a full funeral before cremation, be aware that the funeral home will be completely involved. And they'll love you for it. The minimum you will be paying is for services of the director and staff, transportation from place of death, transportation to the funeral site, possibly transportation to the crematory, embalming, dressing, flower van (utility vehicle), the cremation process, the use of facilities and staff for the funeral service, and the casket. Now, most funeral homes will have a package deal to cover all these items. A cremation casket probably won't be included, but most packages will have an allowance for a cremation casket of your choice. Don't buy a casket. Ask for a discount and use their rental casket. For example, say you want to go for the full meal deal, but don't want to buy that nice cherrywood cremation casket for $1900, even though they gave you an $895 allowance for the casket. Instead, ask for the rental casket (they have one) that according to the funeral home's general price list is available for $695. Then ask for a $200 discount off the package since the rental casket is $200 less than the casket allowance quoted in the package.

Okay, the funeral director has done arrangements for the services and merchandise you want, but you're not finished yet. In walks your at-need cemeterian. He's going to try to sell a gravesite; an urn garden site; a niche; a columbarium; a marker; an urn vault for the above, if necessary; an urn; and, if he's really lucky, prearrangements for all the survivors.

This person will be very nice, and also state that he is very sorry for your loss. Then he will go into how nice it would be to honor your loved one with permanent placement in their cemetery. After all, where else could you go to remember the deceased? In addition, you have the opportunity to build a family heritage, right there in their cemetery for generations to come. All this is true to the extent that you want it to be true. But is it what you want? In other words, are you willing to pay for a space in a cemetery that perhaps no one will visit or even use? On the other hand, do you want to take the chance that Uncle Joe will be forgotten and left in the basement for the next twenty years? I had one family buy niches for Mom and Dad after the daughter discovered Dad's cremated remains behind the washing machine.

It's a matter of your personal feelings and desires, not a matter of what the salesperson thinks. If you're not sure, you can say no and come back at anytime should you change your mind. The best thing about cremation is that it buys you time. Remember, for the salesperson, it's not about the funeral or your loved one; it's about the money. The salesperson is probably on commission only and needs to sell you something, anything. You don't need to buy, if you don't want to. If he can't sell you a niche or an urn garden spot, he'll try to sell an urn. Some cremation packages have an urn allowance, which is designed to make you feel like you're getting some kind of deal. Sure, an urn allowance will be helpful should you choose a cremation package, but what if you want to supply your own urn or you just don't want an urn? If I wanted the cremation package, but had a suitable container at home, I would make them reduce the price of the package by subtracting the urn allowance.

Some places have a stated policy that they won't release cremated remains in the temporary urn (cardboard box) in which the cremated remains are first placed after the cremation process. Instead, you have to either buy an urn or bring a "suitable" container in which to place the cremated remains. This is a sales ploy to get you to buy one of their urns, and it is very unethical. Yet, when a family is informed of this policy, what are they to think? How many families do you know would rush home and bring the cookie jar to the funeral home in which to place grandma? How many families know that the policy is just a sales ploy and that most other funeral homes don't have such a policy? And the funeral home knows this. The law says a funeral home can't make you buy merchandise from their funeral home or any other funeral home. You don't have to buy an urn, and you don't have to bring one from home; you can just take the temporary box and be done with it. If I were presented with such a ploy, I'd demand to get my loved one in the temporary urn, then go somewhere else to buy my urn. Enough about cremations, let's talk funeral.

How does a funeral arrangement differ from a cremation arrangement? Depending on your needs and desires, not by much. One important difference is timing. A funeral must be planned and executed within a reasonable amount of time since the funeral home is not a storage facility. Basically, items that are needed are as follows: the first call, basic services of the director and staff, refrigeration or embalming, the casket, the funeral service, a place of disposition. The devil is in the details.

Be prepared to spend more time at the funeral home arranging for a full funeral as opposed to a cremation. If you have prearranged, you will have taken some very important shortcuts since several of the decisions have already been made. Now, let's go through the nuts and bolts of planning a full-blown funeral.

More than likely, the funeral director will push a package deal. This makes his life easier, and you will probably pay less for the package than if you bought all the items straight from the general price list. The great advantage to the funeral home is that they are likely selling services that you don't want or need. However, the more detailed and expansive the funeral the more a package will make sense. Additionally, should you think of items and services not in the package, the director will be happy to add such items to the bill.

Packages will list everything the funeral home can think of that will make the package look more valuable. Some package deals will include the same items, but will differ only by the casket allowance. In other words, the less expensive package may allow a choice from only two caskets at no extra cost, whereas the most expensive package will allow for a choice from say ten or twelve caskets. Both packages include the same services and items except casket choice. Other funeral homes may present packages that have fewer or differing types of service. For instance, one package may have a funeral service at their chapel or a facility of your choosing, where a less expensive package may only offer a graveside service.

Now you're going to have to make some choices, so let's take them one at a time. For instance, the funeral service itself will require choosing a casket, whether to embalm, music, visitation, pallbearers, memorial folders, perhaps a memorial book, flowers, maybe an organist, clergy, escorts, limousines, a post-service gathering place, and last but not least a formal indoor service or graveside service. We've already have gone through the choice of casket; suffice it to say, it's your choice and your money. Your loved one won't care; therefore, it's a matter of how much you want to spend to impress other people. Should you want to doll up the casket, you can add corner caps to some models. Or, you might want a casket panel which fits on the inside cover of most models. This way your loved one can stare up at a flag or forest for eternity. To some, the casket is an important status symbol; to others, it's not. Remember, the casket will only be on display for visitation, if you have a visitation, and for the funeral and/or the graveside service. After that, it's gone forever.

If you are going to have an open casket funeral or visitation, embalm. Embalming is not required by law, as many people falsely believe; but, if you have the casket open at anytime, embalm. As stated before, cemeteries have certain regulations of their own, one of which is that most mausoleum interments require embalming. Therefore, you have to embalm whether you have an open casket funeral service or not. On the other hand, if you don't want to embalm and it's not a requirement for interment, don't. Most funeral packages will include embalming. But if you think that by refusing embalming you might get the difference back, think again. Because if you refuse embalming, the funeral home will point out that refrigeration charges will apply. I, for one, know that if you have a funeral service and if there is any chance that the casket will be open, you should embalm. I have seen the results of unembalmed remains at a funeral and it's not pretty. No matter how well the make-up is applied to the deceased, things just don't look very good.

Music can be an important part of a funeral service; but it is not required, and it doesn't cost extra. Remember, this is your show. The funeral home can provide appropriate music CDs or tapes for a funeral service, religious or nonreligious, and will go over their music library from which you can pick out what you want and feel would best set the mood. But you might have some favorites of your own that you want played or favorites of the deceased that you feel would be appropriate and appreciated by the attendees. Should the funeral home not have the music you want, you will have to provide the selection. The funeral home will not run out and get Hank William's Greatest Hits just for your husband's funeral. Your funeral director will coordinate with you as to which songs or pieces are to play at what time during the actual service. It will be his responsibility to have the music cued up and ready to play at the appropriate times during the service.

Memorial folders are traditionally passed out to attendees as they enter the place of service, yet memorial folders are not required. Your funeral home will have samples from which to choose. The front cover of the folder will have a picture of trees, a sunset, a lighthouse, or other appropriate image. Inside, on the right, will be the deceased's name, date and place of birth, date and place of death, a schedule of the funeral, the names of the pallbearers (if any), clergy, organist, and other officiates. On the inside left page, you will usually find a quote from a religious text, favorite poems, or some remembrance of the deceased. The funeral home will have examples from which you can choose. The back of the folder can contain more poems or religious sayings or remembrances if you want. Again, remember, whatever is printed on the memorial folder is up to the family members responsible for the funeral itself. Some folks will make their own folders because they don't like any of the examples the funeral home possesses and it gives them a sense of participation. Remember, you don't have to buy from the funeral home. If you choose to make your own, simply supply them to the funeral director prior to the service, and he will hand them out to the mourners.

Memorial books are similar to guest sign-in books you will find at weddings and other functions and again, are not required. As in the memorial folders, the funeral home will have several books to choose from having different front covers depicting sunsets, lighthouses, mountains, and the like. Some books will have a framed slot on the front for a picture of the deceased. Memorial books are good for remembering who attended the funeral service, especially if you want to thank people for attending. It will also remind you of who didn't attend, which will help sharpen the ax you want to grind against certain others later on.

You are not required to get flowers; however, lots of families will arrange for some type of traditional floral arrangement.

Again, the funeral home will have a floral book from which you may choose an arrangement. Floral arrangements, in my mind, are expensive, so don't be too shocked and horrified by the price. You don't have to buy from the funeral home. However, in my experience, all floral shops will charge an arm and a leg for traditional funeral arrangements. But there are no rules; a bouquet of flowers, potted plants, and other simple arrangements are okay. Traditional items, such as easels with lilies and the like or casket blankets, can be costly.

Should you compare prices of floral arrangements between your funeral home and the local flower shops, you will find that they are pretty much the same. However, should you order your flowers through the funeral home, the funeral home will get the arrangements at about ten percent below the listed price presented to you. Thus, the funeral home makes ten percent on the arrangements. Should you want to save a few bucks, you might try going to a floral shop and asking for a ten percent discount. The upside is that you might save some money; the downside is that you are responsible for the floral arrangements and timely delivery of said arrangements. The funeral home knows this and is banking on you being too tired, emotionally involved, and just plain not wanting to hassle with going somewhere else to buy a bunch of lousy flowers. Finally, you can keep or give away all the flowers you've bought or received for the service. Any flowers not taken home after the service will be placed on the grave after burial by the grounds crew.

If you want an organist, soloist, bagpipes, or even a choir, your funeral director will be able to provide these items, at a price. The fee for any of the above is called an honorarium, and the price will vary. For instance, the fee charge by the organist may be fifty dollars, but the funeral home might list the honorarium in its general price list as one hundred dollars. The difference is that some organists might charge fifty dollars, while another might charge seventy-five dollars, and another might require one hundred ten dollars. The funeral home will make some money most of the time, but it may also eat a few bucks once in awhile. The upshot is, how many organists or bagpipers do you know who would be willing to play free at your father's funeral? If you can find an organist cheaper, by all means do so; but my guess is that you're not going to hassle with hunting down an organist just to save twenty-five dollars. Let the funeral home deal with this; after all, that's what you're paying them to do and they have the information at hand.

The same goes with clergy. Almost all funeral services will include clergy. Whether that clergy is Presbyterian, Catholic, Jewish, Muslim, or Buddhist, it doesn't matter; families want clergy.

Now if the deceased went to church on a regular basis, you probably want his or her pastor to do the service. That's good, because the pastor will most likely be able to speak with a little bit of knowledge about the deceased, and you might not have to pay an honorarium to the funeral home. Just give your funeral director his or her name and number, and the director will coordinate with your pastor concerning the details of the service.

However, like many people, the deceased my not be a regular churchgoer. Since death has a lot of religious overtones, clergy are something people attending a funeral expect most of the time; but their presence is not required. In comes your funeral home to the rescue. They have a list of clergy for all religions, denominations or nondenominational. You pay the honorarium, they arrange the clergy. The clergyperson will contact you to get background information on the deceased so that he or she can make a stab at speaking about your loved one without sounding foolish.

Should the deceased be a veteran, he or she is entitled to a military honor guard. Earlier, I talked about national cemeteries and the veteran's right to burial in such a cemetery. But if the deceased is a veteran being buried in a cemetery or memorial park, he or she retains the right to an honor guard and flag. Your funeral director will coordinate with the Veteran's Administration for the honor guard and a flag from (of all places) the post office. However, be aware that you may have to change the date and time of the service to suit the honor guard's schedule; so be flexible.

Escorts? Just say no. Motorcycle escorts are costly, time consuming, and don't work. Unless you have to show people how important the deceased was or you are, escorts are not necessary. If your funeral service is not at the cemetery (as in a combo unit) and you have many people who want to go to the gravesite after the service, have your funeral director hand out directions to the cemetery. Should your funeral procession consist of more that ten cars, the likelihood that the escorts can keep the procession together goes down. To me, it's just not worth it. Ditto for limousines, which are just an extravagant way of getting to and from the service. Again, if you need to show people how much you cared (and how much money you have) or you don't want to drive your grieving mother to your father's funeral, your funeral director will be happy to provide limousines. They will pick you up at your home, get you to the service, drive you out to the graveside, and take you home. All for two hundred and twenty-five to four hundred and fifty dollars per limo. Unless you're incapacitated by grief or old age, don't do it. Better yet—have a friend drive you.

Many families, but not all, hold a post-service reception for the attendees. Most funeral homes have a designated room for such receptions, for a price. The funeral home will not provide food or drink, but will arrange for a caterer if desired. Many families will bring their own food prepared at home. Many families elect to hold the reception at the decedent's or some other family member's home. Some will rent a room at a restaurant, hotel, or even a bar where mourners can hoist a tall one in honor of the dearly departed. The choice is up to you. Holding receptions at the funeral home makes it a bit easier since, right after the services, you can finish it all up and thank people for coming, go home, and not have a kitchen to clean up. But you will pay for the convenience.

As for the place of service, most funeral homes have a nondenominational chapel. Some funeral homes' chapels will accommodate up to three hundred people or more, while others can barely hold forty. Some funeral homes may not have a chapel at all. My funeral home didn't have a chapel. Thus, no overhead

127

was spent maintaining an unused chapel, and a cheaper price was charged for the funeral service. If you examine the general price list of most funeral homes, you will note that the cost of conducting a funeral at the funeral home's chapel as opposed to holding the service elsewhere is usually the same. It is generally cheaper to hold the service in the funeral home's chapel because there will be no rental charge on the building and possible transportation charges. However, if you belong to a church or the deceased was a member of a church, you most likely can hold the service in your church without being charged a fee. It's a matter of preference: do you want to personalize the service by holding the service in a special place or do you want the convenience of using the funeral home's chapel? There is one caveat—some building owners will not allow a funeral to be held within their facility; they don't want a body cluttering up the place.

Let's say you've opted for the simpler and less expensive graveside service. Here you can have almost everything mentioned above with a few exceptions. For instance, it would be very difficult to get your organist and organ out to a graveside service; and you won't need a motorcycle escort since all will arrive directly to the cemetery. But you still can have clergy, music, memorial cards, a memorial book, honor guard, bagpiper, flowers and even a soloist if you so choose. Less time will be spent at a graveside service, it being less formal than a chapel service. At the same time, clergy will eulogize, and others can speak of the deceased if that's what you want. Graveside services are less expensive because the funeral director has less to coordinate. Most funeral homes have both full formal funeral and graveside service packages.

If there has been no visitation, embalming is not necessary for a graveside service unless for some reason the casket is open. Open caskets at graveside services are rare, yet I've seen it done. Lastly, should the weather be inclement, the graveside service might be moved indoors. There the service is held just like it would be at graveside. When finished, all go home and the grounds crew takes over finishing the burial.

All of the above is up to you. You choose what you want and leave behind what you don't want. The funeral director will coordinate all your choices in order for the funeral to come off without a hitch. But be aware, sometimes something will go wrong. For instance, once when I worked for the corporation as a salesman (I was number two in the tag team during the arrangement), the funeral director forgot to place the American flag on the casket for the service of a veteran. The deceased's wife went berserk. This was ten minutes before the service was to begin. The wife of the decedent wanted me and only me to direct the funeral service. The funeral home's manager agreed to let me, as a salesman, direct the funeral. But since I wasn't a licensed funeral director, the manager discreetly placed another director in the background just to make sure I didn't screw up. The missing flag was placed on the casket, and the funeral service went on without any further problems. For the most part, however, most mistakes are small and unnoticed. As a funeral director, you want everything to go right because it only takes one person to make a bad comment on the service, and fifty people will remember the comment. On the other hand, how many people sit around the dinner table remarking on how great the funeral service was for neighbor Joe?

A few words about when to have the funeral service. Most funerals and burials take place three to five days after the death, not counting holidays and Sundays. However, a week is not unusual. When you start pushing more than a week, you might get nailed with extra charges for storage. The more elaborate the funeral, the harder it is to get all the players to agree on a date and time.

In other words, the director needs to coordinate the clergy, organist, honor guard, and other outside providers for the service. This may entail many phone calls to the providers and you in order that all agree on a set time, date, and place. Additionally, should relatives live a great distance from where the funeral is being held and want to attend, there are more people to accommodate.

Should you have people coming from a great distance and need time to arrange for travel, talk to your director about delaying the services. Most funeral homes understand this problem and will try to accommodate you. I knew of a case at one funeral home where the decedent's mother lived in Mexico and had trouble getting a visa in order to attend the funeral. The funeral home stored the decedent for three months without charge; too accommodating in my humble opinion. The point is, ask for things; you just might get them.

By now you should be more aware of the pitfalls and hazards when dealing with a funeral home or cemetery. However, it doesn't stop there. Funeral homes and cemeteries will always figure out a way to separate you from your money. Some of those ways will be in the form of "surcharges," "supplemental charges," and "policy charges." When you're presented with such a charge, ask why. Sometimes the charge will be a legitimate expense that the funeral home or cemetery needs to recover.

For example, you may find that extra transportation outside a thirty-mile radius will have not only the mileage charge but also may have a flat fuel supplemental charge due to the high price of gasoline. Yet charging mileage or a fuel surcharge for getting Aunt Mildred from the funeral home to the crematory is bogus and should be questioned and most likely refused.

One of the best examples of a bogus "fee" occurred upon the death of a friend's grandmother. This lady passed away in one state, but had prearranged, prepaid space and opening and closing of the grave next to her predeceased husband in another state. The family fully realized that they would have to pay a funeral home to ship her remains to the next state and pay another funeral home for receiving those remains. Furthermore, the family had a full-blown funeral service in the receiving state. What they didn't count on was that the cemetery would hit them up for a two hundred dollar "receiving out-of-state body" fee. When my friend consulted me, I said to tell the cemetery to fold it five ways and place it where the moon don't shine. It's a bogus charge. The cemetery wasn't receiving the body directly from an out-of-state funeral home, so there's no extra expense to the cemetery. They were receiving the body from the local funeral home after a service, just like any other body.

The lesson is this: don't accept any charges at face value. Always question. When it comes to your money, there are no dumb questions.

Last, but not least, there's paying for the service. All at-need services are due and payable at the time of the signing of the contract. However, most funeral homes will give you a few days to raise the money if needed. After all, you don't know what the cost for an at-need service and burial will be until you've gone through the final arrangements. Funeral homes take checks, credit cards, cash, and verifiable insurance policies the decedent may have possessed. If you're paying with a life insurance policy, of which the decedent is the insured, the policy must be assignable. For instance, Uncle Joe is the insured of a twenty-five thousand dollar policy. His wife, Sue, is the beneficiary of said policy. She may elect, if the policy allows, assigning a portion of the policy to the mortuary in order to cover the cost of the funeral service and burial. Whether you pay with an insurance policy or cash, you will have to pay and soon.

Unlike prearranged services and goods, a funeral will not give terms for payment on an at-need situation because if you default on payments, the funeral home has little recourse. They can't undo a service, and they can't disinter your loved one and give him or her back. Some funeral homes will give you a little time, maybe up to a month, depending on the situation and how they feel about you. Other homes will demand the money by the time the services are rendered or they will cancel the service. I knew a person whose husband suddenly passed away. Needless to say she was unprepared. Not only did she get browbeaten into spending about fifteen thousand dollars on her husband's funeral service, cemetery, and goods; but also they told her that if she showed up to the service without a check, there would be no service.

The most important point about paying for the service is that the funeral home fears losing your business more than life itself. Therefore, you have no obligations to the funeral home until you sign the sales contract. You can walk away anytime before signing, no feelings hurt, with the exception of any previously authorized charges such as transportation of the body from place of death (first call). Because you can walk at anytime, you have negotiation power. If you've done your homework prior to meeting for the arrangement, you do have them over a barrel. As I've said before, I've had several clients come to my funeral home because the client ultimately figured out that he or she was being lead down the primrose path, in other words, ripped off. This is the ultimate hammer, but don't abuse it. Even a funeral director can get tired of your nitpicking every charge. If you don't ask for discounts, however, you won't receive them.

Be nice: don't go into an arrangement whether pre-need or at-need with a chip on your shoulder. Honey catches more flies than vinegar.

Although obituaries are not part of a funeral or burial service, it is part of the service provided by the funeral director. Some newspapers provide a free obituary service, some provide for a paid obituary, others provide both a free obituary and if desired a paid customized obit. Free obituaries are subject to time and space as the newspaper sees fit. In other words, you may not get the obituary printed on the day you want and the format is fixed. Paid obituaries have a more flexible format and costs are predicated on the space used for the obituary. Since you're paying for the service you can expect the obit to be published on the day you designate. However, don't expect a newspaper to publish an obituary the next day if it's been submitted late afternoon.

Additionally, there are internet obituaries, mostly free, and memorial sites in which people from around the world can express their condolences. Some families have built entire web site around the life and times of their dearly departed one. Many funeral homes provide an internet obituary or memorial web site. Thus, for those who can't make the funeral or burial can acknowledge the death and sympathies to the family. It also is a great advertising tool for the funeral home.

After all is said and done, you will have spent a half-hour to four hours arranging for the funeral. Of course, more time is spent on a more complex funeral. If you as the purchaser are tired, hungry, and emotional with a sprinkling of guilt, you will become a victim. This is why you want to be well-rested and well-fed.

Chapter VIII

The Service and Disposition

"I didn't attend the funeral, but I sent a nice letter saying I approved it."

—*Mark Twain*

Behind the Scenes

The paperwork is done, arrangements made, authorizations signed, and payment received. By this time you should have received any valuables such as jewelry that you don't want buried or cremated with your Aunt Mildred. In the case of cremation, be aware that most knickknacks and jewelry, except for stones, are going to be vaporized. The stone, if large enough, will be crushed in a hammer mill after the cremation. So what happens to Aunt Mildred, who's been patiently waiting in the cooler? Well, it depends. Let's talk about cremation first.

Once the cremation authorization is signed, you have given permission for the funeral home and its representatives to cremate the body. The cremation will take place soon after any preconditions, such as viewing, visitations, and/or funeral services you have chosen. Should the mortuary have its own retort (crematorium), the cremation can take place the same day you met with the funeral director. In most cases, the cremation will take place one to three days after the authorization is signed. Many funeral homes will share a cremation center where bodies from several homes are brought for cremation. This cuts down on the funeral homes' overhead and presumably your cost. These cremation centers are owned by the corporations that own several funeral homes in the area and are not used by independent funeral homes. Additionally, there are independently owned crematoriums, which provide the service for the area's independent mortuaries.

The cremation authorization is sent to the cremation center along with any state-mandated identifying tags (some states mandate identifying tags which match the identifying number on the death certificate). The authorization is checked against the identification on the body. If Aunt Mildred had a pacemaker, it will be removed since it would explode in the retort. Once identification is verified, the body is placed in a cremation container. The cremation container is a seven-foot long cardboard box or cremation casket. The container is placed on a lift and then shoved into the retort. Now, don't worry about Aunt Mildred's gold teeth; it's very unlikely that some schmuck is pulling those teeth with a pair of rusty pliers, although in theory it could happen. The truth is that the gold is low grade, and it's not worth the effort or jail time (abuse of a corpse and theft). The retort is fired up to about eighteen hundred degrees Fahrenheit, thus everything with Aunt Mildred, such as jewelry, will vaporize. And, to answer the question going through your mind right now, no, Aunt Mildred will not sit up and scream when the burners are turned on. There is no room to sit up; and if there were enough air in her lungs to scream, she wouldn't be in the retort in the first place.

After about three hours, all that's left of Aunt Mildred are her bones. These are collected and fed into a small hammer mill. The pulverized bones are then collected into a heavy-duty plastic bag, which is tied off and placed into a cardboard box, which is wrapped in heavy paper and labeled. Should you have picked out an urn, the plastic bag is subsequently transferred to said urn, which in turn is labeled and sealed. Now Aunt Mildred is ready for her memorial service and/or placement on the fire mantle or placement in a cemetery niche. As far as the state is concerned, disposition took place at the crematory.

But what's going to happen to Aunt Mildred if there is a funeral and burial? Again, paperwork needs to be done, in particular the embalming order (if needed and wanted) and burial authorization(s). Should Aunt Mildred be embalmed for visitation and or a service, she will be removed from the cooler and taken to the "prep room." Here the decedent will be cleaned as necessary; and if an autopsy or surgery has been performed, repairs made. Without going into the science of embalming, simply put, the deceased's blood is removed and replaced by embalming fluid. Remember, embalming doesn't stop corruption of the flesh; it merely slows the deterioration down. Aunt Mildred is then dressed with the clothes you provided, her hair is done, and makeup is applied. She is then placed within the casket (casketed) to await the funeral service or visitation.

The Service

You've finished the arrangements, all the players are scheduled and ready, and now the day of the service has arrived. As the responsible party, along with the chief mourners (family), you want to arrive early, but not too early—say around twenty to thirty minutes before the festivities begin. Otherwise, you'll be sitting around waiting. Don't be late because there may be another service scheduled immediately after Aunt Mildred's. This is a good time to set up any photo boards or personal mementos for display at the entrance of the chapel. This day, in my opinion, is going to be the hardest day to get through, assuming you have any feelings for the deceased. Not only is the reality of what has happened going to hit home, but through the funeral service and conversation with friends, you'll be constantly reminded that she is gone, forever. The funeral service is to honor the deceased and put into people's memory the good points about the departed through his or her work, family, and social activities. This is when grief really starts to come forth, which is probably a good thing.

The casket will be in place on what is known as a church truck, open or closed depending on your wishes. All the flowers that have been sent to the funeral home and brought to the service will have been arranged on or around the casket. You, as family, will sit in the front, others behind; and, most likely, appropriate music that you picked out or asked your funeral director to choose will be playing. As mourners file into the place of service, the funeral director and his assistants will be handing out memorial folders. Finally, the music stops and the pastor or whomever you've chosen will begin the festivities. Usually, but not necessarily, prayers will start the service. Next, the pastor will speak about the life of the decedent. If you are using one of the pastors recommended by the funeral home, this portion will be brief since he or she most likely didn't know the decedent.

Music, songs, or hymns will be interspersed throughout the service. A eulogy will be given by the pastor, a family member, or close friend. Many times the pastor or whoever is running the show will ask if any of the mourners wish to speak, provided the family of the deceased has agreed to this. When all is done, exit music will be played, mourners will file out, pallbearers will gather, the flowers will be removed, and the casket will be loaded into the funeral coach. Most services last forty-five minutes to an hour.

However, it's not as simple as that. For instance, when the funeral service is over, many times the mourners will come to the casket to say their last goodbyes, especially if the casket is open during the service. People want to pay their respects, but they also want to see the body. When all have paid their respects, the funeral director will close and lock the casket if necessary. The pallbearers will be given instructions on how to remove the casket, which will then be wheeled out on the church truck and placed in the funeral coach. In the meantime, an assistant will be gathering the flowers to be taken to the grave.

Again, sometimes it's not as simple as just having a service and burial. My most extended funeral service lasted eighteen hours over four days. The services consisted of four hours each for three nights, a four-hour service the day of burial, and two hours at the gravesite. Each service was attended by about three hundred people. Our funeral home had to find a suitable site that could not only accommodate the large number of mourners, their cars, and food for the final day, but was available for four consecutive days. You can guess that this arrangement was due to the religious and cultural needs of the family, and it was what *they* wanted. The entire service was conducted in Laotian, which made it difficult for us to cue the proper music at the right time and open and close the casket at appropriate times as dictated by the family. We also had to break up a fistfight out in the parking lot. Yes, families do fight at a funeral once in awhile. The last day of the service was miserable since I was the only one from my funeral home in attendance; my funeral home was directing two other services the same day. I had to call my brother in to drive the flower car. Once we got to the graveside, there was another two hours spent talking about the decedent. I thought to myself, after all this time what else could be said about the deceased? Yet, it all went off without a hitch, and I charged the family about one-third what another funeral homes would have charged and still made a profit. The point is that you don't have to have a "normal" service; make it what you want. The funeral director should be accommodating; if not, go somewhere else. Of course, be prepared to pay more if you want more.

If you insist on a procession with motorcycle escorts, they will be waiting outside the place of service. Once the casket is loaded, it's off to the cemetery. Don't ask to go in the funeral coach. It's not a place for family members and is considered an out-of-the-box (no pun intended) request. Sometimes the funeral director will give a lift to the pastor as a courtesy, especially if the pastor has been retained directly through the funeral home. However, most of you will not choose to have a procession; the mourners will go directly to their cars. It's okay to follow the coach to the cemetery—that way you'll know where in the cemetery to park. Sometimes the family will elect not to have a graveside ceremony, in which case family and friends will either attend a reception or just go home. Meanwhile, Aunt Mildred goes to the cemetery as a "delivery only" (D.O.).

Graveside services can be held for full-body burial, inurnment, or placement in a mausoleum crypt directly following a funeral service. What has become popular is a graveside service in lieu of a funeral service. After you and your director have determined place and time of a graveside service, your funeral director or the family services counselor (second member of the tag team) will contact the cemetery and grounds crew, sending a copy of the burial authorization, the exact grave, and the time of the service. (You may have to be flexible as to scheduling.) The grounds crew will most likely open the grave the day before the service or at least several hours before the service. Using a backhoe to dig the grave, they will dig up to six feet down; however, most are about four to five feet deep. The grave will be seven feet long. There is no room for error since each grave is surveyed down to the inch. I have seen open graves where the liner or vault from the grave next to the open grave is visible. Next, the grounds crew will put the grave liner into the grave, place the lid off to the side, lay some support bars across the grave to hold the casket, and in most cases remove the dirt out of sight. Usually an awning and chairs will be set up for the chief mourners with artificial turf set around the grave to give a more aesthetic look.

If you purchased a grave vault, the vault company will deliver the vault shortly before the graveside service, place the container in the grave, and hold the lid aside nearby. The vault company will have to hang around until after the service in order to place the lid on the vault. After all, it weighs about eight hundred pounds. This is why timing is so important to the funeral director. Not only does he have to end the service in the allotted time, he must get everyone to the graveside at the correct time because if the vault company is held over too long, the vault company will charge the funeral home overtime. Many families opt for a graveside service only for several reasons: a) some funeral homes will offer a graveside service for less than a chapel service, b) there will not be many people attending, therefore a chapel service seems inappropriate, and c) it's simple and less formal. However, you can make it as formal as you want. For instance, you may have a bagpiper, other live music, or a military honor guard. Your funeral director will arrange all that you want, for a price (the honor guard is free).

After all have assembled for the graveside service, the pastor or whomever is appointed will say some words, followed by whatever the family wants, such as inviting people to speak about the deceased. Mostly, it's just the pastor who speaks and that will be the end of that. Once, it was raining so hard, that the family simply drove as close to the grave as possible, and the pastor said a few words from his car. No one got out of their cars, and when the pastor finished his bit, everyone drove away, leaving myself and the grounds crew to lay the deceased to rest. Finally, when all is said and done, the funeral director will step forward and say something like, "This concludes the service; on behalf of the family and our mortuary, thank you for attending." People will start drifting away although some will linger.

Disposition

Now there are some choices to make. For instance, which, if any, of the flowers do you wish to take home or give away? The funeral director and his staff should help load them in your car. Do you want to stay for the closing of the grave? While all this is going on, someone from the cemetery will act as sexton. The word *sexton* ultimately comes from the Latin *sacristanus* meaning *keeper of sacred objects*. In years gone by, the sexton was the caretaker of the church buildings and graveyard and the actual gravedigger, but now is probably the family-service counselor who sold you the grave and cemetery accoutrements. The sexton will sign county papers attesting that the person in the casket actually is buried in the grave.

The closing of the grave is a simple affair. The grounds crew will take down the awning, remove the chairs, move the flowers out of the way, and roll up the artificial turf. Next, with two people on each side, two wide straps will be placed under the casket in such a way that two people on each side of the casket can lift and lower the casket. When all is ready, the four people will slightly lift the casket so that a fifth person can remove the support bars from under the casket. Without further ado, the casket is lowered into the liner, which is already in the grave. The liner lid is attached to the backhoe and lowered onto the liner. Dirt is brought in and dumped into the grave. Then the backhoe is run across the grave in order to tamp down the soil. Sod that was cut away when the grave was open is replaced, as are any flowers the family didn't take with them.

I was always less enthusiastic about families watching the grave closing. Families watching backhoes or other equipment running over the fresh grave of a loved one never appealed to me. Also, the grounds crew may be dirty from other work in the cemetery, which doesn't add to the solemnity of the event. Should the cemetery be soggy after rain, things can get messy to the point where the grounds crew may have to lay planking down in order that the equipment doesn't tear up the entire cemetery. Finally, on rare occasions, something can go wrong, such as dropping the casket or breaking the liner lid as it's being placed on the liner. As a funeral director, you don't want the family around as any problems are being corrected. However, as a funeral director, you can't deny the family the right to watch.

Should you have decided to spend more money than necessary and purchased a burial vault, the closing is a little different. First, as you gather for the graveside service, you'll notice that the vault is suspended over the grave, unlike a liner which is already inserted into the grave. When the casket arrives for the service, it is also suspended over the vault by means of two supporting bars. The lid to the vault is placed nearby so that all can see how you spent your money.

After the service is completed, the grounds crew, along with a worker from the vault company, removes the awning and chairs. The vault company worker has to stay around for the end of the service since he has specialized equipment designed to lower the vault and its lid into the grave. Supporting bars are removed and the casket is lowered into the vault. The vault company's special equipment picks up the lid to the vault, brings it over the vault and grave, and lowers the lid onto the vault. The lowering mechanism then is attached to the vault, which is first raised so that the vault's supporting bars are removed, then lowered into the grave. Finally, the grave is closed in the manner described above.

For some extra money, about one hundred and fifty to two hundred dollars, the vault company will use an automatic lowering device. In this case, the vault is suspended over the grave resting on the mechanism. The lid is also on the mechanism. When the graveside service is completed, the casket, which has been suspended over the vault is lowered into the vault, the lid automatically slides over the vault, and then the vault is lowered by the mechanism into the grave. This is a way for all the mourners to watch the casket and vault lowered into the grave without having to get up from their seats. If I wanted to see my loved one lowered into his or her grave, I'd let the grounds crew remove the awning, seats, and artificial turf, stand back, and just watch. That way I'd be about two hundred dollars better off.

A graveside or crypt-side service may be held in a mausoleum. You may find less room for mourners to gather at a crypt-side service because you are dealing with a building, but for the most part everyone can jam into the area. A crypt-side service is just like a graveside service except in the opening and closing of the crypt. Upon arrival, the mourners will find a hole at the location of the crypt. The grounds crew has already removed the facing of the crypt, usually marble or granite. The casket is placed on the church truck and rolled next to the designated crypt. After the service, should you desire to watch, the grounds crew will bring in a lift should the crypt be higher than the second tier of crypts, place the casket on the lift, raise the lift to the crypt opening, and shove the casket into place. After the casket is pushed to the rear of the crypt, a piece of Styrofoam or cardboard is placed over the crypt opening and caulked into place; then the crypt facing is brought up, placed, and sealed by means of four screws. That's why the opening and closing for a crypt is less expensive: no heavy equipment, less personnel, and less time spent on the operation.

Ditto for niche-side services and interments. Of course, these are even easier for opening and closing because size does matter, and they are therefore also less expensive. Here, we are only placing an urn into a small niche—no lifts are required, maybe just a ladder. Should you have a niche or garden urn spot at a cemetery, it is important that the urn fits into the niche and/or that garden urn spot you picked out. Additionally, should you pick out a "glass front niche," in other words a niche that displays your urn and other memorabilia, then most cemeteries reserve the right to reject your urn should it prove to be unsuitable for display (another way to get you to buy the urn from them.) Lastly, most cemeteries will not allow you to place the temporary urn you received from the crematory in the ground or a niche.

Now, if Aunt Mildred is to be cremated and she already has a niche with Uncle Harry, but you don't want any services, go with a direct cremation and a "delivery only" interment. The funeral home should not charge you for the direct cremation plus an immediate burial fee. Should a funeral home try to charge for both services, don't walk out; run. They might try to charge you a transportation fee to deliver the cremated remains to the cemetery, but that's baloney. If the cemetery is nearby or across town, they should deliver the remains without charge as a courtesy. However, if they are delivering the remains across country, be prepared to shell out about fifty dollars for postage. That's right; they mail cremated remains to either family or cemeteries for final placement.

Say your aunt suddenly dies, you are the only family, and she has no friends to speak of, or at least none that can escape from the nursing home to attend her service. Her husband died several years ago and is planted in the local cemetery, where a space awaits your aunt. After shopping around, you decide on a funeral home (you didn't like the one your aunt used for your uncle), telling the funeral director you don't want any services whatsoever, just "get 'er done." Well, the immediate or direct burial is just your ticket. Also known as a "delivery only" (D.O.), it's the cheap way to bury, and if you're not having any services, it's the way to go. It's the cheap, quick, no-witnessed burial for the family on the go. You're going to pay anywhere from about four hundred to twelve hundred, depending on the funeral home. This gets you the services of the funeral director and staff, transportation from the place of death to the funeral home, refrigeration, arrangement of permits, and transportation to the place of burial. Some places will charge you extra for an embalming should the burial be in a mausoleum crypt; some places will include embalming. You shop, you decide.

Remember, for an immediate burial, you're going to need a casket. Since no one will be witnessing this event, there's no reason on God's green earth to invest much money in a casket. Think back to the example I gave where I arranged to move an already deceased husband to a new double crypt, to remove him from his old casket, and to sell two copper caskets—one for him and one for his wife to use upon her demise. What a tremendous waste of money. No one saw the caskets except the funeral home staff. As far as anyone is concerned, those two caskets could be made from plywood; no one would care. The lesson is, if you're going to have a cheap burial, think cheap casket.

Chapter IX

Some Different Burials and a Disinterment

"I'm a rocket man."

—*Elton John*

Remember, the arrangements for burial and a funeral are your show. There are no restrictions on anything allowed by law. Your funeral director or pre-need salesperson will be delighted to arrange almost anything you want. A good salesperson will ask questions in order to get you to open up and reveal your real desires. Never mind that those desires may be outlandish or cost prohibitive. Many of my clients would say, "I can do that?" Well sure, for a price.

So you've always wondered what it would be like in space; or your father was an Air Force pilot, but didn't make the astronaut program. Well here's his or your chance: space burial. Yep, your dad can fly to the stars without all the training, education, and danger. The excitement and sensation of weightlessness may be lost on the deceased, but if you think it would be "cool" and a good way to memorialize, by all means, go for it.

In order to shoot the moon, the deceased must be cremated. Full-body outer space burials are not done since the weight of a corpse would make the trip cost-prohibitive, at least for now. The cremated remains are just part of a payload of other equipment.

Additionally, not all of the deceased's cremated remains get to launch, just one to seven grams are packed in a small capsule the size of a lipstick container. Once the rocket reaches orbit, the capsule is released to circle the earth every one-and-a-half hours or so. Over time, the orbiting capsule will slow and be pulled back to earth, whereupon the capsule will burn up re-entering the earth's atmosphere. Now the deceased becomes a shooting star, which no one will notice or see, all for about five hundred dollars.

If you want to pay much more, you can place your father on a probe, say to the moon or Mars. But if you feel he needs to explore the universe, he can go for space flight that's going beyond Pluto. The further out you go, the more you pay. A funeral home and its director will be needed for the cremation, but the flight arrangements should be done by family; otherwise, the funeral home will be adding something extra to the bill for making the arrangements. For my money, I'll keep my feet, or what's left of me, on *terra firma*, but if you need more information I suggest going to memorialspaceflights.com.

Sea Burials

No, sea burials these days are not the same as in the days of wooden ships and men of iron. If you're hoping Dad will be buried at sea wrapped in a canvas bag with a nine-pound iron ball at his feet, sliding out from under a flag with pipes a-twittering and dropping into the water—well, it's not going to happen. Most sea burials consist of scattering cremated remains over a body of water. Many companies will do this for you for a fee. They will even play the music and say any prayers or poems that you designate; but at the low end of the price list, you don't get to attend. For more money, you can make a cruise of it,; but why not just take a cruise? Why not get your own boat, or hire one and do it yourself? Biodegradable urns are available should one want to toss Aunt Mildred onto the briny sea; they float until the urn disintegrates. Most people will just open the urn or container and scatter. The scattering should take place on the leeward side of the boat or Aunt Mildred might blow right back on board.

It is possible to have a full-body burial at sea. However, a full-body burial is a lengthy and expensive business. Permits have to be granted, the casket has to be of a type that will sink directly and rapidly, and the burial must take place in a certain depth of water. The Coast Guard doesn't want floating caskets or bodies littering the ocean and creating a navigation hazard. Again, I'll stay on dry land; for me, it's too much hassle and too wet. Of course, a funeral director is needed for body prep and delivery to the vessel. And you'll pay for it. Not only will you be charged for all the regular services, there also will be an up-charge to arrange for the sea burial. But worst, you'll pay the funeral director to learn how to arrange for a full-body sea burial since very few funeral homes have ever done one before.

Green Burials

For those of you who feel the need to lie in repose *au naturel*, then the green burial is made for you. Unfortunately, green burials have not swept the country like wild fire. At the time of this writing, places that accommodate people who want to get back to Mother Earth lickety-split, are few and far between. That being said, more and more cemeteries and funeral homes are positioning themselves in order to pick up this market should demand rise. After all, no funeral home wants to leave any money on the table.

A green burial can be as formal or informal as desired, the difference being at the cemetery. The cemetery is a "natural" setting, usually in the woods. You will not see pathways or any evidence of graves. What you will see is nature. There are no burial vaults to buy, usually no markers to fret about, and the caskets are either plain plywood boxes or made from a papier-mâché type of material for quick bioremediation. In some places a burial shroud is acceptable. A hole is dug, the deceased is wrapped in a shroud or placed in a paper box, and then lowered into the hole and covered up. The family gets the

147

Global Positioning coordinates in order to locate the deceased in subsequent years.

This doesn't mean that you can toss Grandpa in the backyard and call it a green burial. Municipalities have strict ordinances concerning burial grounds. Even green burial cemeteries have to be permitted as a cemetery or memorial park. A few memorial parks and cemeteries that were built for traditional burial are now designating a portion of their cemetery to green burials. In these cases the cemetery has designated an undeveloped portion of their park and instead of developing the grounds in a traditional cemetery style, they've just surveyed the gravesites and are selling those graves for green burial. In other words, you can find a few cemeteries/memorial parks that do both traditional and green burials; however, good luck in finding a green burial cemetery within one hundred miles of your home. I prefer the traditional burial site, but that's just me. It's a matter of choice.

Disinterment

There is no truth in the belief that you can only be buried once. Disinterment and exhumations, although not common, do occur from time to time for various reasons. Exhumation is usually the disinterment of a body for legal reasons, such as performing an autopsy. In some cases, the family will request an autopsy or reexamination of the remains in order to prove something or other. Once in awhile the court will order exhumation due to a challenge in court or the reopening of a criminal case. Most exhumations end in reburial of the deceased in the same spot as he or she was exhumed. The exception is exhumation followed by cremation. I've never done an exhumation followed by cremation, and I think it is rare in this country. However, in some countries, such as Argentina, this is very common.

Disinterment is the same as exhumation but with the general understanding that the deceased will be reburied in another spot. Disinterment as well as exhumation, which is the actual process of removing the body from the grave or crypt, will require a funeral director. Let's say your Uncle Joe died twenty years ago and is buried in Nevada. Subsequently, Aunt Mary has moved to Florida, wants to be buried in the Sunshine State, and wants her dear departed husband to join her in the land of hurricanes. What's a person to do? First, the only person who can exhume, disinter, and rebury is the one who has legal control over the body and interment. This prevents anyone from willy-nilly digging up bodies and moving them all over the country without a court order. Here, Aunt Mary has all the rights in the world to move Uncle Joe, and she wants you to arrange for the disinterment. Again, shop, shop, and shop. You will need a funeral home to arrange for the disinterment and do the transfer. Essentially, this is a burial in reverse, but you might need new merchandise. The funeral director will interface with the cemetery, fill out any paperwork for the county, state, and cemetery, and, if need be, transfer remains into a new casket. When arranging for a disinterment, the funeral director will want your Aunt Mary's John Hancock on a disinterment authorization; that's first. Next, he's going to go over the charges just as in a burial arrangement. He or she will want to push merchandise and even a service if the director can squeeze one out of you. What you're going to get nailed for is services of the director and staff; a new casket, depending on the condition of the old casket; an air tray if the remains will be shipped by air; opening and closing of the grave; transportation to the new gravesite; opening and closing of the new grave; new grave liner; and receiving charges at the funeral home handling the reinterment.

There are a couple of things you need to be aware of when exhuming a body. Should Uncle Joe be buried in a vault, then, when disinterring Uncle Joe, the casket he lies in and the burial vault can all be put on a truck and shipped to the new cemetery. However, if he's in a grave liner, which by this time has filled with water on several occasions, and in a wooden casket, he will need a new casket from the removing funeral home and a new grave liner from the receiving cemetery. The way to negotiate the disinterment is to not pay and negotiate individual items on the general price list, but to negotiate against the price of "forwarding remains to another funeral home," plus whatever merchandise you might need (casket, air tray, etc.). This gets you all the paperwork and Uncle Joe on the airplane or truck. The opening and closing of the grave is the only charge you should see from the exhuming cemetery itself. If you have to buy a new casket, the funeral director might try to hit you for casketing and disinfecting charges. Should you be told that you have to pay for casketing, threaten to take your business somewhere else. Casketing should be included in the cost of "forwarding of remains."

If the funeral director tries to charge for "disinfecting of remains," just say no. The funeral home personnel are not going to mess with Uncle Joe. They will transfer the remains into a new casket, maybe using the old casket's bedding in order to transfer Uncle Joe in one piece. The funeral director doesn't want to mess with Uncle Joe any more than you do; therefore, "disinfecting of remains" is a bogus fee, in my mind. Should your funeral director try to sell another service in order to "honor" Uncle Joe, leave. That would be ridiculous. The director is just trying to pump up the sale; the process has nothing to do with Uncle Joe. Don't forget to ship Uncle Joe's marker. The cemetery will handle this through your funeral director. There may or may not be a small charge for handling. But there will be a charge for shipping.

My first disinterment was of a child who died at the age of ten. The family had moved from the area, and they wanted to rebury their child near their new home. The funeral director charged them fifty dollars for services of the director and staff and opening and closing of the grave (it was very small), plus three hundred and fifty dollars for a new child's casket. In my mind, this was fair and right. The director filled out some paperwork, oversaw the opening of the grave (yes, he actually attended), supervised the transfer of remains to the new casket, and helped load the new casket and old casket into the family's vehicle. Yes, the family self-transported and even took procession of the old casket to use as a flower planter. After all, they paid for the old casket at the time of their child's death, and they had every right to keep the thing. They also had every right to transport their child's remains; so do you.

For Uncle Joe, the funeral home in Florida will charge you for "receiving remains from another funeral home." This will get Uncle Joe from the airport to the cemetery. The cemetery will charge you for the gravesite and the opening and closing. They may even charge you for setting Uncle Joe's marker; but since you're buying a new gravesite from them, possibly two, since Aunt Mary will eventually need one as well, you might get them to set the marker free. It doesn't hurt to ask. The receiving funeral home may also try to sell a service; say, "No, thanks."

Remember, your duty is not to Uncle Joe—it's to Aunt Mary. If you're arranging a disinterment and burial, it's your fundamental responsibility to guard Aunt Mary's money and emotional well-being. A final point: you may desire to witness the disinterment and reburial. That's all well and good; however, the funeral homes involved may charge extra because you are making them schedule an event, in other words, a service. It is my advice to let them exhume, transfer, ship, and bury without witnessing. Let the receiving funeral home transfer from airport or truck directly to the cemetery as a "delivery only" in order to avoid any service charges. You can still watch unofficially.

Finally, not only have you bought two new plots for Aunt Mary and Uncle Joe, you have two plots from the cemetery you just vacated. Those old plots are in control of Aunt Mary. She can choose to give them away or sell them, but she is unlikely to return them to the cemetery. Cemeteries rarely buy back inventory they have already sold once. Should they do so, they would deeply discount the value, and they would only do so for plots in sections of the cemetery that are expensive and in high demand. Aunt Mary's best choice would be to give or sell them to family members. Barring that, she could sell them on the open market under (way under) the price for which the cemetery is selling gravesites in the same section. I don't recommend using a cemetery broker although they are running around out there. I've never heard a good word about brokers, and there's a good chance that you won't hear from them after they take your up-front "brokerage" fee.

Chapter X

Controlling the Industry

"Don't fence me in."

—Cole Porter

This work is intended to educate and to demonstrate how to work with a mortuary or cemetery. I've covered what I think is necessary in order for you to be confident that you will know what you want and don't want. I've given examples to demonstrate what is necessary and what is superfluous. That being said, one might wonder if there is a way to clean up the industry and make it more consumer friendly. For what they are worth, I give my ideas and opinions below.

Aside from the laws prohibiting fraud and theft, I, for one, am not a great supporter of government rules and regulations. That is not to say government doesn't have a stake in funeral industry oversight; it does. But to have government sticking its finger in all aspects of the industry would only make the industry less efficient, corrupt, and more costly. When government starts regulating, it costs the individual funeral home more to operate. Regulations take away choices for the operator and the consumer. The responsibility for a fair and good purchase lies with the buyer. The buyer must be informed and educated as to what he or she is purchasing. A smart customer is a happy customer because that customer knows what he or she is purchasing, why he or she is receiving the product or service, and if he or she is getting a reasonable price.

It's the uninformed who gets ripped off, comes away dissatisfied, and complains.

It is important to understand that the funeral industry is a business and needs to make a profit. Profit is what motivates all of us. They are not servicing the needs of your family out of the goodness of their hearts. It's not about the funeral; they're there to make money. In my opinion, the funeral industry needs to make some changes in its thinking, mainly to risk short-term profits for long-term gain, in other words, realize the consumer is going to get smarter and know more about the industry. Understanding growing consumer awareness and positioning themselves as the providers of consumer needs and desires could and should achieve a long-term gain for the industry.

I do have opinions on some changes that need to take place in order for the industry to be consumer friendly and make a decent profit. A big step to improve the image of the death care industry would be a general housecleaning, as well as improving the professional deportment of the staff at each unit. Most funeral directors possess an associate of arts degree or higher. Many states require this education level. Unfortunately, entry level as a funeral director hardly supports the idea of a four-year bachelor of arts or science degree; the pay is simply too low. However, every funeral home should strive for this education level. A four-year degree doesn't guarantee the production of an ethical professional, but it does widen one's experiences and presumably matures the mind. Secondly, all salespersons should be required to possess an associate of arts degree. The degree can be in any field, but the industry should require that all personnel be able to read, write, and speak the language of this country. The sales manager, if the mortuary possess one, should be required to have a four-year degree. One thing which should never be tolerated is a dirty, poorly spoken, untrained staff member who is allowed to come near a customer. It doesn't matter that the customer may be poorly spoken and poorly dressed—he's the customer! The funeral home staff should treat all customers with respect and should present themselves as such. Bear in mind, I advocate voluntary changes. Forced change can be oppressive change.

Aside from getting rid of the commission structure, funeral home/cemetery management should get rid of the ne'er-do-wells. There is no reason on God's green earth to hire or retain a staff member who has demonstrated bad ethics and consistently bad judgment, fails to perform duties on time or properly, uses drugs, or steals a coworker's leads. I've seen too many instances whereby the guilty are overlooked for the sake of possible future revenues. Management is only shooting itself in the foot. People now sue at the drop of a dime, and unprofessional staff only opens the door for such suits. It is unbelievable to me that a guy snorting cocaine out in the parking lot can be hailed as the champion salesperson.

Some have even suggested that government pay for burials and cremations. That would ruin the industry and eliminate any choices you may want. With government, there are strings and conditions. The costs will rise, service will be diminished, and mistakes will be made without accountability. Why would you want to pay for the burial of Joe Blow across the state? There is no free lunch, and a government takeover will cost everybody. To quote Benjamin Franklin, "The only sure things in life are death and taxes." Why do we want to combine the two?

Therefore, what should be the role of government? Simply put, oversight. The federal government has no business in the funeral business. Sure, forcing standardization of the general price list through the FTC was a good thing. This was the big move by the Feds to eliminate fraud in the funeral business. All it really did was to standardize the pricing format, something the funeral and cemetery industry should have done years ago on its own. I can't for the life of me understand why the industry doesn't want to eliminate fraud when and where it can. Oversight should be left exclusively to state and county governments and should be strictly limited. It is important to restrict government's meddling because the more government meddles, the more it will cost you. Then someone in government will decide that it's unfair that one family can have a certain casket or service when others can't afford the same. That kind of thinking will restrict services and merchandise available, thus restricting your freedom of choice. Be that as it may, state and local government can play a very important role in oversight in three ways.

First, the government should have complete and thorough access to any documents, records, and information concerning trust accounts. One of the major issues the public has with the death care industry is trust accounts that disappear. This issue has plagued the industry since trust accounts were set up for prearranged funerals. Holding trust funds is the one thing that large corporations have over the independents; should some schmuck embezzle trust funds from one of their local affiliates, the corporation will cover the loss. After all, they don't want to lose their billion dollar business because some jerk of an employee ripped off one hundred thousand dollars from the corporation's trust fund. Embezzling funeral and cemetery trust funds can be big business. Recently one person was convicted and another jailed and awaiting trial for the embezzlement of almost one hundred million dollars. And what were they going to do with the money? Buy more cemeteries. Talk about robbing Peter to pay Paul!

Government, without notice, should be able to examine and, if necessary, audit all trust fund accounts funeral homes are holding for their clients. Funeral homes and cemeteries should report on an annual basis how much money they have in trust funds and where the money is being held. That way if there is a large dip in the number of trust funds they're holding, a red flag would go up at the appropriate state agency. Funeral homes and cemeteries should report immediately any suspected fraud or embezzlement of such funds; and if they try to cover up, criminal chargers and/or fines should be slapped against any and all who participate in such a cover-up. Better yet, these trusts should be held by a third-party trust company, such as a bank.

Secondly, the state should have powers of certification, licensing, and testing of facilities and personnel. All funeral homes and cemeteries should be certified as to being a funeral home, a cemetery, or both. This certification process should be easy, since it is my belief that should one who is qualified, such as a funeral director, desire to open and own a funeral home, more power to him or her. However, a funeral home should be exactly that, and a cemetery should not be opened in your next-door neighbor's backyard. Additionally, the state should license cemetery and funeral personnel by administering the appropriate test(s) and background investigations. It is my firm belief that no license or certification be issued to anyone having a criminal record whether it's for an embalming license or a pre-need salesman.

Thirdly, the government should enforce all state and local laws and regulations. By this, I mean the government should enforce and punish those that break the rules. Funeral directors and embalmers know the laws and regulations; they have to in order to pass the state examination. Pre-need salespeople should be trained and taught the laws pertaining to their livelihood. These people, when they willfully and knowingly break the laws and regulations, should be hammered and hammered hard. For instance, a pre-need salesperson sold a marker to a party that was paying in cash. Instead of handing the cash and a contract for the marker over to the cemetery, she pocketed the money and trashed the contract. The customer found out that there was no contract for the marker when he went to the cemetery to make a change on the marker's design. Since the cemetery had no record of a marker being bought but now had the customer's copy of the contract, the problem was easily traced back to the salesperson. The customer made a formal complaint to the state's mortuary and cemetery board. What did they do? Suspended her pre-need sales license for one year. One year? Her license should have been revoked, and she should not be allowed back into the death care industry. As for the funeral home, they fired her two weeks after they discovered the theft from their own company. They should have had her arrested; it's ridiculous.

State mortuary and cemetery boards have a powerful enforcement tool that is not used—newspapers and the Internet. These boards or agencies should post on their websites and publish in the local newspapers all violations of which a funeral home, cemetery, or personnel working for such are found guilty. That way, the public can be notified (by newspaper) or easily find (by Internet) those organizations in the business that are violating laws and regulations. It would motivate the industry to keep its nose clean because the last thing they want is more damage to their reputation than they already have. When those found guilty of violations are publicly exposed, other employees would motivate each other to avoid violations since no one wants some schmuck working at the next desk to ruin the reputation of the organization; it's bad for business.

Before I Go, What I Know

The funeral industry is big business and doesn't care one iota about your funeral. It does care about your money. As such, the industry is willing to provide you with goods and services in order to separate you from your money. As in all purchases, the more educated you are about the item or service to be purchased, the more likely you will be to make a purchase that benefits both sides.

As in all businesses, there are corrupt people just as there are also the straightforward, honest salespeople only interested in making a deal that will pay their wages and make you pleased with your purchase. It is your duty as the consumer to find those who will deal with you in an honest straightforward manner. Some shopping, common sense, and a little moxie will get you a long way with any purchase you make.

The funeral industry is at a crossroads. With cremation rates on the rise and body burials becoming less frequent, the industry must change in order to achieve long-term survival. One path much of the industry seems to want to take is to make cremation a special event in order to charge more, thereby covering more of the overhead once covered by the cost of full-body funeral services. Other funeral homes and companies, recognizing the new cremation trends, are offering low-cost services in order to capitalize on this current movement to cremation. The choice is for you to make; maybe you want an "event" where money is no object. On the other hand, maybe simplicity is for you. Either way, you must become knowledgeable about what you want and what you want to purchase. After all, it's your funeral.

My best wishes to all; may the road be flat and the wind at our back as we all march to our inevitable future.

LaVergne, TN USA
26 November 2009
165392LV00002B/9/P